The Macat Library

世界思想宝库钥匙丛书

解析查尔斯·P. 金德尔伯格

《疯狂、惊恐和崩溃：金融危机史》

AN ANALYSIS OF

CHARLES P. KINDLEBERGER'S

MANIAS, PANICS, AND CRASHES

A History of Financial Crises

Nick Burton ◎ 著

陈汉敏 ◎ 译

上海外语教育出版社
SHANGHAI FOREIGN LANGUAGE EDUCATION PRESS

目　录

CONTENTS

引言

要 点

- 查尔斯·普尔·金德尔伯格是美国经济学家，出生于 1910 年，于 2003 年去世，享年 92 岁。

- 他的著作《疯狂、惊恐和崩溃》（1978）分析了过去和现在的金融危机 * 的本质。

- 《疯狂、惊恐和崩溃》认为市场具有内在不稳定性，这源自非理性行为和信贷供应的激增。

查尔斯·P. 金德尔伯格其人

　　《疯狂、惊恐和崩溃：金融危机史》（1978）的作者查尔斯·普尔·金德尔伯格 1910 年出生于纽约市。在他杰出的经济学家和学者职业生涯中，他反对 20 世纪 70 年代的传统经济学思想，认为世界金融市场并不像人们想象的那样有序和有效 *。金德尔伯格断言，市场不稳定，容易出现危机，有时需要激进的干预措施。

　　金德尔伯格的职业生涯始于宾夕法尼亚大学和哥伦比亚大学的经济学 * 学位，并在哥大获得了博士头衔。在第二次世界大战 * 前后（1939—1945），他曾为美国政府工作，并帮助起草了马歇尔计划 *。二战期间，欧洲的基础设施和工业遭到严重破坏，这项计划支援了欧洲的重建。他于 1948 年加入麻省理工学院经济系担任教职。

　　在他的经济思想中，金德尔伯格追求国际视野；他是最早认识到各个国家的经济相互依存的思想家之一。在 20 世纪 70 年代，他注意到国际经济中的某些变化，他认为这些变化可能会助长波动（即不稳定）和金融危机。他在经济危机发展过程中观察到的模式为他最具影响力的思想奠定了基础。

金德尔伯格有丰富的经济史 * 知识，并使用文学化、叙事化的风格写作，这与同代学者惯用的数学分析完全相左。《疯狂、惊恐和崩溃》阐述了 20 世纪 70 年代被重新唤醒的全球经济 * 的内在不稳定性。从这个意义上说，他的书具有预见性，预测了许多 21 世纪的金融灾难，如 2008 年的金融危机 *。

《疯狂、惊恐和崩溃》的主要内容

《疯狂、惊恐和崩溃》是一部经济史的经典作品，它研究了大量过去的金融危机。这些例子支撑了金德尔伯格的理论观点：每次金融危机都不是独一无二的。纵观历史，这些危机有很多共同之处。这些一致的特征和发展阶段是金德尔伯格所谓的"生物规律性" *，可以通过对经济史的研究来解码。[1] 一旦理解了这一点，经济政策的制定就可以用来最小化这种混乱造成的损害。

金德尔伯格在《疯狂、惊恐和崩溃》中的观点拒斥了 20 世纪 70 年代流行的经济效率模型。这是一种假设投资者理性的理论，即那些希望从后续投资中获利的资本提供者会基于理性而行动。相反，金德尔伯格将金融危机视为这些市场参与者中的俗众心理的结果。一种近于"疯狂"的强烈乐观情绪通常来自信贷供应激增的煽动，而金德尔伯格则认为这是一个核心问题。轻松获得信贷使投资者能够通过债务购买资产 *，在对价格上涨的过度乐观的"狂热"预期中，这些投资者陷入巨额债务——同时还在假设其资产价格将永远保持上涨。

当这些资产的价格停止上涨（这是不可避免的）时，就会突然出现"恐慌"，导致资产价值"崩溃"。由于贷款未得到偿还，银行和其他金融机构可能会破产，他们自己也会负债累累。然后，一波破产可以通过国际传染＊而立即蔓延到好多个国家。例如，如果投资者从墨西哥银行借入大量资金而无法偿还，墨西哥的银行可能会破产。美国可能在墨西哥银行投入过大量资金，如今无法被偿还，也只能面临突如其来的破产。英国银行也许根本没有在墨西哥投资，但在美国银行拥有巨额资金。因此，墨西哥的危机最终可能会导致破坏英国银行的连锁反应。为了说明这一点，金德尔伯格引用了19世纪经济学家阿尔弗雷德·马歇尔＊的话，"鲁莽交易的祸害总会蔓延到直接相关者之外。"[2] 这正是世界经济如此脆弱的主要原因。

在《疯狂、惊恐和崩溃》中，金德尔伯格认为人们无法阻止这样的危机；人们只能控制它们。他认为，需要有一个国家能够为全球经济运行负责，并在动荡期间稳定全球经济。在第一次世界大战＊（1914—1918）之后，当英国作为一个全球大国的角色逐渐消退时，他认为美国应该担当起这个角色。

《疯狂、惊恐和崩溃》的学术价值

《疯狂、惊恐和崩溃》是对金融危机运作方式的著名而精辟的分析。它首版于1978年，当时世界正进入全球经济脆弱的新时期。资本主义＊（主导西方并逐渐扩散到全球的经济和社会体制，其中的商业经营以追求私人利润为导向）历史上共有过10次大繁荣和大萧条的交替，其中6次发生在接下来的40年间。金德尔伯格的著作持续受欢迎的程度表明，国际金融危机仍然是世界经济的首要问题。自2003年金德尔伯格去世以后，经济学家罗伯特·Z.阿利伯＊编辑并更新了《疯狂、惊恐和崩溃》的后续版本。

金德尔伯格的文本不但非常及时，纵观金融危机的悠久历史，他创作了一部轻松愉悦的作品，传达了关于市场固有不稳定性的严肃学术观点。他认为这种波动性永远不会消失，只能进行积极管控。投资者的非理性行为是历久不变的，今天仍然普遍存在。

1978年，经济学家的传统思想基于市场理性的假设，即像银行家和投资者这样受自我利益驱动的市场参与者能做出理性的选择。金德尔伯格坚持认定非理性投资行为的持续存在——这在1978年属于非正统的立场。从那时起，探讨非理性投资决策并将心理学*纳入经济模型的全新的经济研究领域开始出现（特别是行为经济学*领域）。这些领域已经涌现了不少诺贝尔奖*得主，包括罗伯特·J.希勒*，金德尔伯格的学生之一，他形容后者"对他的思想产生了巨大的影响"。[3]

在学术界之外，金德尔伯格的著作也影响了政治家和政策制定者，其中一些人已经应对了多次全球金融危机。对任何有志于了解市场周期性繁荣和萧条*的人来说，《疯狂、惊恐和崩溃》如今是必读书目。作品风格也很新颖，金德尔伯格文学化的叙事方式与经济学文本中常见的数学和模型不同，这使得《疯狂、惊恐和崩溃》成了一本引人入胜的读物，一个关于人的故事。

---

1. 查尔斯·P.金德尔伯格和罗伯特·Z.阿利伯：《疯狂、惊恐和崩溃：金融危机史》，贝辛斯托克：帕尔格雷夫·麦克米伦出版社，2015年，第20页。
2. 金德尔伯格和阿利伯：《疯狂、惊恐和崩溃》，第56页。
3. 罗伯特·J.希勒：《非理性繁荣》，普林斯顿：普利斯顿大学出版社，2015年，第92页。

第一部分：学术渊源

1 作者生平与历史背景

要点 🗝

- 《疯狂、惊恐和崩溃：金融危机史》描述了金融危机的广阔历史，呈现了关于其产生原因的可信理论。

- 金德尔伯格于二战前后（1939—1945）在美国政府的工作经历强化了他的学术教育背景。

- 20 世纪 70 年代重燃的世界经济动荡引起金德尔伯格的密切关注，使他感到提出书中想法的迫切需要。

为什么要读这部著作？

查尔斯·P. 金德尔伯格的《疯狂、惊恐和崩溃：金融危机史》初版于 1978 年，现在已经是第 7 版。它成为经济学史上的经典巨著，到现在还被全世界的学术界，金融家、政治家和新闻记者广泛引用。

这本书描述了金融危机的全景历史，一直可追溯到商业活动诞生之初。金德尔伯格详细描述了金融危机发生阶段的共性，在叙述过程中，他声称并非所有的危机都是独一无二的，它们实际上具有一种"生物规律性"，能够反映出市场具有从繁荣到萧条波动的内在趋势，这一循环在特定阶段不断重演。[1] 在开始阶段，某项来自外部的冲击或"移位"* 导致经济扩张，商业公司的乐观情绪"高涨"，投资因为信贷容易获得而激增。[2] 证券 *（股票、债券和期权等金融产品）价格和房地产价格大幅上涨，一直到另一次冲击——也许是政府政策的变化——导致这些价格停止上涨，转而引发崩溃："那里没有高原，也没有'中间地带'……出售这些证券的热潮变得不言而喻、刻不容缓，以至于就像一场恐慌。"[3]

虽然他对金融危机的解剖并非完全原创，但金德尔伯格是最早将此类事件置于国际背景下的学者，他提供了与当今全球经济日益相关的新见解。正如美国经济学家罗伯特·M.索洛*在他为第7版所作的序言中说的那样，"读罢本书，任何一位读者都会获得这样一个鲜明的观念：世界各地大量的流动资本飙升应该会大大增加它们泛滥四溢的可能性。"[4]金德尔伯格的论证提供了减缓或最小化（如果不是消除）此类金融危机的潜在解决方案，为当今政治经济中的这一紧迫问题做出了重要贡献。

> "就银行业危机的数量、范围和严重程度而言，自20世纪80年代初以来的30年是货币史上最为动荡的30年。"
> —— 查尔斯·金德尔伯格：《疯狂、惊恐和崩溃：金融危机史》

作者生平

查尔斯·金德尔伯格出生于1910年。他于1932年毕业于宾夕法尼亚大学，1937年获得哥伦比亚大学经济学博士学位，在货币理论家詹姆斯·W.安吉尔的指导下学习。值得注意的是，金德尔伯格的本科教育发生在大萧条*时期，一个始于20世纪20年代后期的、前所未有的金融混乱时期。

在第二次世界大战期间服役后，金德尔伯格于1945年至1947年成为美国国务院*德国和奥地利经济事务部主任，并于1947年至1948年担任欧洲复兴计划的顾问。在担任顾问一职时，他帮助设计并实施了马歇尔计划，这是美国在战后为重振欧洲经济所做的巨大努力。这些角色与经历为金德尔伯格的学术背景增添了政策制定的实践经验，有人认为这有助于金德尔伯格形成他在《疯狂、惊恐和崩溃》中所描述的思想——特别是他秉持的"国家和国际机构可以稳定全球经济"的论点。[5]

1948年，金德尔伯格在麻省理工学院开始了他的经济学学术生涯，直到1976年从首席教授的职位上退休。在此期间，他多次担任美国政府顾问，出版了大量书籍和文章。他持续关注国际领域的金融危机研究，最终贡献了两大经典著作：《大萧条的世界，1929—1939》（1973年首版）与《疯狂、惊恐和崩溃》（1978）。

创作背景

金德尔伯格在大萧条时期接受了经济学的教育。在他的学术课题中，一场关于到底是什么原因导致这场经济灾难的激烈辩论延续了几十年。德高望重的经济学家们提出了他们各自（非常不同）的理论。例如，英国经济学家约翰·梅纳德·凯恩斯*表示，这个问题是因为长期缺乏消费者需求所致，应由增加政府支出来支撑。美国经济学家米尔顿·弗里德曼*认为，原因是美国联邦储备系统*（美国中央银行*）未能向银行提供额外资金以满足存款人的需求。数十年后，金德尔伯格也将被吸引到这个重大议题上，他将提供更加国际化的分析。他认为，在第一次世界大战（1914—1918）之后，英国作为国际经济领导者的角色逐渐消退，这恰恰是在全世界经济格局最需要它的时候，而与此同时，美国却不愿承担这项任务。由此产生的真空使世界陷入大萧条。

第二次世界大战后，金德尔伯格在重建世界经济期间为美国政府工作。在20世纪50和60年代，他目睹了全球经济相对稳定的状态——但已发生的一些基础性的变化令他非常担忧。20世纪70

年代的早期国际经济已经显得非常不稳定，商品（可交换物品）、货币、债券、股票*（商业中的可交易份额）和房地产每日每月的价格相对它们的长期平均价格发生着巨大变化。[6]新技术显然在这方面发挥了作用：通信和计算方面的创新意味着资金可以更加积极地在世界各地流动，即使是冲着很小的预期增量收益，投资者*也可以将资金转移到外国的金融中心。[7]这些快速的资本*流动只会刺激泡沫*，当资产（房地产）或证券（作为上市公司所有权凭证的金融协议）的价格以经济基本面无法解释的方式快速上升时，"泡沫"就产生了。[8]

金德尔伯格意识到一种新的全球不稳定性正在产生，让人联想起那个导致大萧条的时代，他开始根据历史先例对其进行研究，成果就是《疯狂、惊恐和崩溃》。

1. 查尔斯·P.金德尔伯格和罗伯特·Z.阿利伯：《疯狂、惊恐和崩溃：金融危机史》，贝辛斯托克：帕尔格雷夫·麦克米伦出版社，2015年，第20页。
2. 金德尔伯格和阿利伯：《疯狂、惊恐和崩溃》，第104页。
3. 金德尔伯格和阿利伯：《疯狂、惊恐和崩溃》，第20页。
4. 金德尔伯格和阿利伯：《疯狂、惊恐和崩溃》，第VIII页。
5. 斯蒂芬·梅尔顿："谈金德尔伯格与霸权：从柏林到麻省理工及其归程"，鲍登数字共享，2013年9月29日，登录日期2016年3月22日，http://digitalcommons.bowdoin.edu/cgi/viewcontent.cgi?article=1003&context=econpapers。
6. 金德尔伯格和阿利伯：《疯狂、惊恐和崩溃》，第5页。
7. 金德尔伯格和阿利伯：《疯狂、惊恐和崩溃》，第25页。
8. 金德尔伯格和阿利伯：《疯狂、惊恐和崩溃》，第43页。

2 学术背景

要点 🔑

• 当金德尔伯格撰写《疯狂、惊恐和崩溃》时，经济管理部门主要受制于理性行为和有效市场假说理论，也就是认为资产价格是准确的价值指标的理论。

• 对于有效市场假说*的拥护者来说，国际贸易提升市场效率，任何动荡都是该过程的一部分。

• 金德尔伯格拒绝接受这一假设，转而关注国际投资中的非理性因素，它们助长了不稳定性。

著作语境

查尔斯·P.金德尔伯格在20世纪70年代撰写了第1版《疯狂、惊恐和崩溃：金融危机史》。当时，研究金融市场的大多数经济学家都接受有效市场假说的理论，这种理论的最纯粹形式排除了泡沫的可能性，所谓泡沫就是诸如房地产或证券的资产定价过高，会导致经济上的风险。[1]

这些经济学家有充分的理由。以诺贝尔奖获得者E.F.法玛*和著名的普林斯顿大学教授伯顿·G.马尔基尔*为代表的有效市场假说理论的拥护者认为，证券价格充分体现了相关公司的所有可获取的新闻和信息。如果股价不是如此，即意味着定价不正确，人们会蜂拥而至利用这种定价不均（通过购买或出售价格不合理的股票），导致无效的市场迅速消失。因此，利用这种市场的无效性赚取大量收益或多或少是不可能的。同样的逻辑排除了金融泡沫的可能性，有效市场假说理论将过去的泡沫归咎于未成熟的、充满欺诈的市场，并断言这种泡沫不太可能发生在成熟的、监管良好的现代市场中。[2] 金德尔伯格在《疯狂、惊恐和崩溃》中提出相反的观点，认为完全非理性的行为经常主导市场，并造成金融危机。

金德尔伯格也是他那一代经济学家中少数几个对在 20 世纪 50 和 60 年代占主导地位的"货币主义者"*（如米尔顿·弗里德曼）持怀疑态度的经济学家之一。[3] 他们认为经济的表现主要受货币供应量的影响。对于货币主义者来说，如果限制货币供应量（例如通过提高利率），便可以控制泡沫的产生。而金德尔伯格认为，大部分房地产或股票价格泡沫的产生是由于信贷供给的激增和国际投资的流入。[4]

> "失去与理性的联系反映出投资者、贷款人、借款人及银行和金融监管机构未能认识到崩溃始终是狂热的结局。"
>
> —— 查尔斯·金德尔伯格：《疯狂、惊恐和崩溃：金融危机史》

学科概览

金德尔伯格的研究揭示了一些著名思想家从事金融危机主题研究的历史渊源，以及政府或中央银行如何能够遏制金融危机的历史背景。他描述了丰富多彩的当代和历史事件，所有事件都集中在证券和房地产价格的各种飙升以及随后由此引发的崩溃上。[5] 金德尔伯格经常引用"古典经济学家"*（18 和 19 世纪开创了市场经济理论的一批经济学家）的理论。这个群体包括经济学家和哲学家约翰·斯图尔特·穆勒*和经济学家沃尔特·白芝浩*这两位创立市场不稳定性概念的英国人，金德尔伯格在他们的基础上展开研究。[6]

例如，穆勒首先提出了一个家庭、企业和政府在一定时间内可以获得多少信贷的问题。[7]这个问题成为金德尔伯格研究的一个核心。他还一直引用"白芝浩原则"*，认为中央银行必须在危机期间以惩罚利率向有偿付能力的银行提供无限量的信贷（这种"惩罚"确保中央银行真正被用作"最后贷款人"*）。[8]金德尔伯格进一步推动这一想法，认为此类帮助还必须包括资不抵债的银行（无法返还客户所投现金的银行）。[9]

金德尔伯格写作之时，有效市场假说理论正处于其广为流行的高峰期。在他看来，这个理论的核心是"理性预期"的假设：投资者对经济变量的变化作出反应，仿佛他们能够充分知道每一个变化的长期影响。[10]对于金德尔伯格来说，这个想法完全被历史所否定："理性是关于世界应该如何运作的先验假设，而不是对世界实际运行方式的描述。"[11]

学术渊源

有效市场假说在20世纪70年代广受欢迎，经济学家海曼·明斯基*的"金融不稳定假说"*（20世纪60年代发展起来）显得有些过时。这是可以理解的，因为他基本持相反的观点：市场经济中的金融系统在本质上是不稳定的、脆弱的、容易发生危机的。[12]明斯基以信用周期理论支持这一观点，这可能是对金德尔伯格这本书的主要影响。从本质上讲，明斯基认为信贷供给具有顺周期性*：即信贷供给的增加延长了经济繁荣的扩张，而信贷供应的减少加剧了随后的崩溃。[13]"明斯基模型"*是一个解释过去和现在的金融危机非常实用的工具，因为许多金融危机都是信贷供应增加导致房地产价格飙升的结果。[14]

　　明斯基模型遵循同样让金德尔伯格感兴趣的古典经济学家的传统，[15] 特别是市场不稳定的"经典"观念；这些早期的经济学家使用像"过度贸易"这样的术语来描述狂热，说它导致了"反感"期（恐慌），并最终导致"失信"（崩溃）。他们还专注于研究信贷供给的变化，这是后来被明斯基放大的研究议题。金德尔伯格可以被视为这个思想学派的最近成员，他将此传统学派的理论研究置于更加国际化的背景之中。

1. 《经济学人》，"谈疯狂、惊恐和崩溃"，2003 年 7 月 19 日，登录日期 2016 年 3 月 22 日，http://www.economist.com/node/1923462。

2. 《经济学人》，"谈疯狂、惊恐和崩溃"。

3. 查尔斯·P. 金德尔伯格和罗伯特·Z. 阿利伯：《疯狂、惊恐和崩溃：金融危机史》，贝辛斯托克：帕尔格雷夫·麦克米伦出版社，2015 年，第 2 页。

4. 金德尔伯格和阿利伯：《疯狂、惊恐和崩溃》，第 25 页。

5. 金德尔伯格和阿利伯：《疯狂、惊恐和崩溃》，第 25 页。

6. 金德尔伯格和阿利伯：《疯狂、惊恐和崩溃》，第 27 页。

7. 金德尔伯格和阿利伯：《疯狂、惊恐和崩溃》，第 85 页。

8. 金德尔伯格和阿利伯：《疯狂、惊恐和崩溃》，第 278 页。

9. 金德尔伯格和阿利伯：《疯狂、惊恐和崩溃》，第 323 页。

10. 金德尔伯格和阿利伯：《疯狂、惊恐和崩溃》，第 53 页。

11. 金德尔伯格和阿利伯：《疯狂、惊恐和崩溃》，第 55 页。

12. 金德尔伯格和阿利伯：《疯狂、惊恐和崩溃》，第 27 页。

13. 金德尔伯格和阿利伯：《疯狂、惊恐和崩溃》，第 2 页。

14. 金德尔伯格和阿利伯：《疯狂、惊恐和崩溃》，第 27 页。

15. 金德尔伯格和阿利伯：《疯狂、惊恐和崩溃》，第 39 页。

3 主导命题

要点 🗝

- 20 世纪 70 年代中期与金德尔伯格同时代的学者关注的主要问题是市场如何促成有效的结果。

- 许多经济学家就 20 世纪 20 年代末和 30 年代大萧条时期灾难性经济衰退的原因进行辩论,他们遵从英国经济学家约翰·梅纳德·凯恩斯的"需求驱动"理论(根据此理论,可以通过政府支出的方式振兴不景气的经济),或美国经济学家米尔顿·弗里德曼的货币供应理论(根据此理论,可以通过控制流通中的货币数量来稳定经济)。

- 金德尔伯格以更加国际化的视野看待大萧条的成因,认为世界经济最近的发展会导致更大程度的不稳定。

核心问题

查尔斯·P. 金德尔伯格在《疯狂、惊恐和崩溃:金融危机史》中寻求回答的核心问题是:为什么会发生金融危机?为何现在看起来金融危机越来越严重,越来越普遍?那人们可以做些什么呢?"如果许多金融危机都有一种程式化的形式,"他问道,"是否应该有标准的政策回应?"[1]

金德尔伯格看到过去和现在的大多数泡沫都受到信贷供应激增的影响,但也有一个全球脆弱性的新来源是他这个时代所特有的。全球"支付失衡"*发生于 20 世纪 60 年代后期,并持续到后来的几十年。[2] 为了解释支付失衡的原因,我们可以考虑沙特阿拉伯的例子。

在 20 世纪 70 年代，为了抬升国际油价，提高石油生产商的利润率，世界上许多顶级产油国都赞同有意减少原油产量。产油国沙特阿拉伯向其他国家的出口远远超过进口，这导致它与进口石油的国家之间存在巨大的"支付失衡"。沙特阿拉伯与这些国家进行贸易所获得的巨额顺差*可以在全球投资以获得进一步的回报，目标可以是沙特首选的任何资产——比如他们可以投资泰国证券（股票等可交易资产），在某天市场价格被推高之后突然卖出，再将收益投资于巴西证券——或者是当时有吸引力的任何其他全球性投资。

因此，这种流动的资金在世界各地寻找更高的利润形成"跨境投资流"*（跨越国界的金融安排，通常采取贷款、收购或信贷的形式）。跨境投资流动存在巨大的货币问题。[3] 如果来自世界各地的资金涌入巴西股市，巴西货币本身也会升值。如果巴西证券价格达到顶峰，市场预期不再有丰厚回报，那么所有这些全球投资者可能会立即将其出售，导致巴西证券价格和货币价格的崩溃。为了尽力在遭遇不可避免的快速贬值（价值损失）之前能抛售他们的资产，投资者会突然蜂拥跑路。因此，这种投资流动可能造成一个国家同时面临金融危机**和**货币危机。[*4]

> "然而，尽管各个时期缺乏完美的可比性，但毋庸置疑的结论是银行业危机已经变得更为广泛和普遍。"
> —— 查尔斯·金德尔伯格：《疯狂、惊恐和崩溃：金融危机史》

参与者

有效市场假说理论（包括股票价格在内的资产价格能够反映

关于该资产的所有可用信息）的支持者在 20 世纪 70 年代的经济管理部门中非常普遍。他们认为这些跨境投资流动反映了长期的全球效率。他们认为，全球资金正在全球范围内良性运转，很可能会流向价值被低估的投资，从而将价格提高到有效均衡的水平，同时降低那些价值较低的投资价格（这里的"均衡"指的是资产价格的定价，反映资产真实的、均衡的价值）。这可能是一个颠簸的过程，但只要让国际市场运作，不受经济监管 * 阻碍，就可以实现稳定。

像米尔顿·弗里德曼那样的货币主义者（那些认为宏观经济的市场表现与货币流通数量密切相关的人）承认市场可能会有过热的危险，把利率 *（借贷的价格）作为一种实现市场稳定性的手段。例如，如果政府可以通过提高利率来控制国内货币供应，它就可以抑制过度通胀的市场：较高的利息会提高借贷的成本，所以愿意借贷的人会变少。最终，这可以降低整个经济体的需求。正如金德尔伯格所说，"许多货币主义者坚持认为，过去的许多（乃至大多数）周期性困难都是由于货币管理机制不善造成的。"[5]

过去几十年的一系列金融危机加剧了这场辩论的激烈程度，越来越多的声音加入其中。经济学家罗伯特·Z. 阿利伯在金德尔伯格过世后接替了编辑和更新《疯狂、惊恐和崩溃》的角色，他在第 7 版中指出，2008 年的全球金融危机以及随之而来的经济衰退催生了一连串有关该主题的书籍。它们大多由 3 种作者撰写：财经记者、学者和从事金融工作的"内部人士"。[6] 总体而言，这些新作没给阿利伯留下太多印象，"这些书大多有这样一个缺点：它们没有解释为什么危机会在那个时候发生，也没有解释为什么有些国家被牵连其中，而其他国家却没有。"[7]

当代论战

与同时代流行的理论形成鲜明对比的是，金德尔伯格对金融危机的本质有截然不同的看法。根据经济学家海曼·明斯基相对不太受欢迎的金融不稳定性假设理论，经济繁荣会导致鲁莽的投资行为，金德尔伯格发展了明斯基的观点，即鲁莽地使用信贷周期会导致狂热、恐慌和不可避免的崩溃。

《疯狂、惊恐和崩溃》首次出版后不久就出现了又一波全球金融危机，这时有效市场理论的权威已经开始减弱。例如，丹尼尔·卡内曼*和阿莫斯·特沃斯基*——人类意识和经济行为领域的研究人员——于 1979 年发表了一项关于"行为决策理论"的研究，声称投资者对预测未来股票价格和企业收益的能力有系统性的过度自信。[8] 他们的结论预示着行为金融学*的出现，一个转向心理学以回答经济行为问题的学科领域，这向有效市场假说理论提出了严肃挑战，同时也支撑着金德尔伯格关于投资者的非理性"乌合之众"行为的观点。

即便如此，当《疯狂、惊恐和崩溃》于 1978 年首次出版时，弗里德曼的货币主义仍然是主要决策者的信条，从 1979 年到 1982 年，美联储（美国中央银行）开始限制货币供应量的增长，努力遏制美国经济的高通胀*（货币价值下降，价格上涨），这种努力被称为伟大的"货币主义实验"，并且有了明显喜忧参半的结果。[9] 尽管如此，货币工具（大体来说，就是控制经济中货币供应的措施）仍然非常受欢迎，并且仍然被视为一种强大的手段，用来平息商业周期中从繁荣到萧条的更大波动。

最后，1978 年还有经济学家和著名的舆论导向者声称加强监管是防止金融危机的方法——事实上，**总**有人提出这种说法。[10] 金德尔伯格实际上不同意这一政策，他所声明的理由近乎异端：让银行等金融机构对金融危机负责就是将"危机的症状错认为是动因"。[11] 在金德尔伯格看来，即使**要**这些公司对崩溃负责，银行业"也难以规范，因为会规避监管的新机构不断出现"。[12]

---

1. 查尔斯·P.金德尔伯格和罗伯特·Z.阿利伯：《疯狂、惊恐和崩溃：金融危机史》，贝辛斯托克：帕尔格雷夫·麦克米伦出版社，2015年，第235页。

2. 金德尔伯格和阿利伯：《疯狂、惊恐和崩溃》，第219页。

3. 金德尔伯格和阿利伯：《疯狂、惊恐和崩溃》，第220页。

4. 金德尔伯格和阿利伯：《疯狂、惊恐和崩溃》，第222页。

5. 金德尔伯格和阿利伯：《疯狂、惊恐和崩溃》，第28页。

6. 金德尔伯格和阿利伯：《疯狂、惊恐和崩溃》，第16—17页。

7. 金德尔伯格和阿利伯：《疯狂、惊恐和崩溃》，第17页。

8. 伯顿·G.马尔基尔："有效市场假说及其批评者"，《经济学视角期刊》第17卷，2003年冬季刊第1期，第63页。

9. 大卫·R.哈克斯和大卫·C.罗斯："1979—1982年的货币政策实验：货币主义者、反货币主义者，或伪货币主义者？"，《后凯恩斯经济学期刊》第15卷，1992—1993年冬季刊第2期，第281—288页。

10. 金德尔伯格和阿利伯：《疯狂、惊恐和崩溃》，第239页。

11. 金德尔伯格和阿利伯：《疯狂、惊恐和崩溃》，第3页。

12. 金德尔伯格和阿利伯：《疯狂、惊恐和崩溃》，第28页。

4 作者贡献

要点 ⚯━

- 金德尔伯格断言，非理性的投资行为和信贷供应的激增会造成金融危机，然后传播到全世界。
- 金德尔伯格的论点很大程度上借鉴了经济学家海曼·明斯基的"金融不稳定假说"，该理论认为金融危机源于经济繁荣时期信贷供给的增加。
- 《疯狂、惊恐和崩溃》作为第一本从国际视角审视金融崩溃的著作开辟了新天地。

作者目标

　　查尔斯·P. 金德尔伯格的《疯狂、惊恐和崩溃：金融危机史》的主要目标是审判经济学的"理性假设"："核心的问题是证券和房地产市场是否总具有理性，或投机是否会导致不稳定性。"[1] 对于金德尔伯格来说，投资者总是"理性"行事的想法显然只是一个神话，已经被纯粹的历史事实所揭穿。那些不相信他的人，比如有效市场理论的追随者——认为只要让市场自由运行，金融市场的资产价格最终能反映他们的真实价值——仿佛生活在一个幻想世界里。[2]

　　金德尔伯格旨在证明"狂热"（盲目抢购金融产品，哄抬价格）的成因是在经济繁荣时期信贷和跨境投资流（比如贷款或收购的财务安排）的激增。[3] 不可避免的是，潮流会转向，证券和房地产（依赖宽松的信贷政策推动）价格开始下跌，引发"恐慌"，然后"崩溃"。[4] 最后，金德尔伯格表明这个已经发展到全球范围的问题没有简单的解决方案。[5]他最终建议设置国际层面的"最后贷款人"制度——由一家金融机构（或整个国家）为全球的银行提供救助，从而防止全球金融体系的崩溃。[6]

金德尔伯格还有一个目的是揭示投资者的非理性行为与他们所使用的金融机构之间的联系，因为这种非理性行为似乎很大程度上取决于这种联系。[7]例如，他指出在经济显得"亢奋"时，并不只有投资者是过度乐观的，"这些权威机构意识到有些不同寻常的现象正在发生，虽然对早前的狂热还心有余悸，但他们还是会说什么'今时不同往日'，并给出充足的理由。"[8]就在不久以前，戈登·布朗*先生——彼时的英国财政大臣（财政部长）——刚刚宣布"繁荣与萧条周期的正式结束"。[9]2008年全球金融危机就证明了这个伟大的声明是多么的错误。

> "信贷的普遍崩溃，无论时间多短，都比最可怕的地震更可怕。"
>
> —— 米歇尔·舍瓦利耶：《北美信札》

研究方法

金德尔伯格的方法与有影响力的英国进化理论家查尔斯·达尔文*的方法有些相似，他通过"收集、检验和分类金融混乱历史中的有趣标本"展开研究。[10]可以说，金德尔伯格并未有意挑选那些支持他先入为主的立场的"标本"，而是根据历史事实形成他的论点。[11]他最终得出了一种独特的且独具洞察力的论述，揭示了金融危机根本和统一的原因。

同经济学前辈海曼·明斯基一样，金德尔伯格的理论基石是强调信贷供给变化的"顺周期性"。[12] 这意味着在经济周期的上升期，当投资者对未来的财务前景感到"亢奋"时，信贷资源变得更加丰富而容易获得；[13] 当亢奋开始消退，经济衰退开始出现时（就像 2007 年美国信贷紧缩 * 时，信贷变得难以获得），信贷供应大幅减少而加剧最终到来的崩溃，使整个金融系统面临破产的威胁。[14] 正是这种观点使得金德尔伯格提出国际性"最后贷款人"的解决方法，来提供为防止金融崩溃所需要的财政援助。

时代贡献

经常会有人批评金德尔伯格的论点并非完全原创。[15] 认为经济体的信贷供给是繁荣与萧条主要来源的"明斯基模型"，在金德尔伯格的著作之前已存在良久。金德尔伯格的原创性在于将这种观点扩展到国际背景，例如，他指出"俄亥俄州的银行破产会导致汉堡和斯堪的纳维亚的信贷短缺"。[16] 金德尔伯格希望揭示金融危机的国际传染性，正如"历史上群情狂热经常从一个国家传播到另一个国家"，它们所导致的恐慌和崩溃也一样。[17] 金德尔伯格全球视角的另一个例子是他对国际货币投机者 * 的清楚认知，当某国的经济周期从繁荣转为萧条时，这些人经常抛售该国货币，这会因货币危机而加剧该国的金融危机———一国货币的贬值将劝退潜在的投资者（以及带来其他后果）。

金德尔伯格扩展了明斯基的观点，他更详细地研究了金融危机的各个阶段。首先出现的是"移位"，在此期间取消对银行业务或投资的监管导致繁荣，或者新技术和创新从根本上提高了市场的盈利能力（比如在互联网发明后的 20 世纪 90 年代后期，信息技术的繁荣带来互联网公司的投资激增）。[18] 这通常会导致投资价格的上涨，产生一种"亢奋"情绪，吸引更多投资者。[19] 再就是寻求利润的投机者的加入推动超高价格的"狂热"，直到出现一个标志着繁荣结束的重大事件：如银行或大公司的倒闭。[20] 随后就是"剧变"的阶段了，出现了大规模的恐慌性抛售和价格暴跌。[21] 这是一个从历史中得出的理论框架，但金德尔伯格以其初现时的新鲜感探究理论的精确度。事实证明，在这一点上他与学者、金融家和政策制定者有相当的共鸣。

---

1. 查尔斯·P. 金德尔伯格和罗伯特·Z. 阿利伯：《疯狂、惊恐和崩溃：金融危机史》，贝辛斯托克：帕尔格雷夫·麦克米伦出版社，2015年，第27页。

2. 金德尔伯格和阿利伯：《疯狂、惊恐和崩溃》，第55页。

3. 金德尔伯格和阿利伯：《疯狂、惊恐和崩溃》，第31、78、201页。

4. 金德尔伯格和阿利伯：《疯狂、惊恐和崩溃》，第20页。

5. 金德尔伯格和阿利伯：《疯狂、惊恐和崩溃》，第23页。

6. 金德尔伯格和阿利伯：《疯狂、惊恐和崩溃》，第279页。

7. 金德尔伯格和阿利伯：《疯狂、惊恐和崩溃》，第vii页。

8. 金德尔伯格和阿利伯：《疯狂、惊恐和崩溃》，第41页。

9. 詹姆斯·柯卡普："戈登·布朗承认他错误地宣称自己结束了'繁荣和萧条'的交替"，《电讯报》，2008年11月21日，登录日期2016年3月22日，http://www.telegraph.co.uk/finance/recession/3497533/Gordon-Brown-admits-he-was-wrong-to-claim-he-had-ended-boom-and-bust.html。

10. 金德尔伯格和阿利伯：《疯狂、惊恐和崩溃》，第vii页。

11. 金德尔伯格和阿利伯：《疯狂、惊恐和崩溃》，第vii页。

12. 金德尔伯格和阿利伯：《疯狂、惊恐和崩溃》，第1页。

13. 金德尔伯格和阿利伯：《疯狂、惊恐和崩溃》，第84、104页。

14. 金德尔伯格和阿利伯：《疯狂、惊恐和崩溃》，第 1、245 页。

15. 《经济学人》，"谈疯狂、惊恐和崩溃"，2003 年 7 月 19 日，登录日期 2016 年 3 月 22 日，http://www.economist.com/node/1923462。

16. 金德尔伯格和阿利伯：《疯狂、惊恐和崩溃》，第 2 页。

17. 金德尔伯格和阿利伯：《疯狂、惊恐和崩溃》，第 44 页。

18. 金德尔伯格和阿利伯：《疯狂、惊恐和崩溃》，第 72 页。

19. 金德尔伯格和阿利伯：《疯狂、惊恐和崩溃》，第 41 页。

20. 金德尔伯格和阿利伯：《疯狂、惊恐和崩溃》，第 46 页。

21. 金德尔伯格和阿利伯：《疯狂、惊恐和崩溃》，第 46 页。

第二部分：学术思想

5 思想主脉

要点 ⟜—ⴳ

- 金德尔伯格将他的研究重点放在投资者的非理性行为、信贷激增、跨国投资流动，以及投资狂热如何迅速变成恐慌然后造成崩溃上。

- 通过大量的历史实例，金德尔伯格推论金融危机具有"生物规律"，表明它们具有相同的发展阶段；然后他提出为控制金融危机可以采取哪些措施。

- 金德尔伯格认为经济学领域已经变得太数学化了；他用带有强烈叙事色彩的"文学经济学"、以人文的语言表述他的观点。

核心主题

查尔斯·P. 金德尔伯格的《疯狂、惊恐和崩溃：金融危机史》指出了导致重大经济崩溃的共同因素：投资者的非理性行为、信贷激增、跨国投资流动和迅速变成恐慌及后续崩溃的投资狂热。金德尔伯格发现，股票和房地产价格的暴涨往往伴随着信贷供应和跨国投资流动的激增。[1] 他还研究了权威货币机构（每个国家的中央银行）与私营银行和贷款人之间的关系。他得出结论说，问题不在于大型银行不受监管，而是资金太容易借贷。[2] 如此宽松的货币环境使得银行自己创造更多的信贷，购买更多的贷款，最终当乐观狂热变成惊恐与崩溃时，银行就会破产。[3]

金德尔伯格还剖析了繁荣和萧条的各个阶段。从一个国家的房地产或股票市场内的乐观兴奋情绪开始，投机者借入越来越多的钱进行更多投资，希望获得可观的短期收益。只要信贷容易获得，这些专业投机者总是能够借更多的钱来支付未偿还贷款的利息。一个不祥的问题在金德尔伯格的论述中一次又一次地得到回应："如果没有足够的新贷款来提供资金，那么借款人将从哪里获得资金来支付未偿债务的利息？"[4] 这引出了他的最后一个主题："最后贷款人"的重要性。在当今的全球经济中，需要在国际层面上为大型银行和公司提供所需的救助，以防止或减少它们的失败对整个经济的连锁影响。

> "每一次疯狂在模式上都有其相似的生物规律，尽管细节上有所差异。"
> —— 查尔斯·P. 金德尔伯格：《疯狂、惊恐和崩溃：金融危机史》

思想探究

金德尔伯格认为狂热根本无法被阻止。一旦金融界的"内部人士"（有权获得最新趋势的投资者）开始在特定市场上赚钱，不久后，"随着其他的公司和家庭看到投资者们赚得盆满钵满，一个跟风的过程就发展起来了。"这背后的原因是情绪化的，而不是理性的；"没有什么比看到一个朋友发了财更加扰动一个人的幸福感和判断力了，除非这发财的人不是朋友。"[5] 这些外来者（金德尔伯格的"非朋友"）把他们的钱也投进去，随着势头发展，很快就形成泡沫了。[6] 这时如果信贷很容易获得，人们会疯狂借贷，以充分利用市场的繁荣——相信这次好机会会持续很久（因为"今时不同往日"）。[7] 这种鲁莽更加推动了泡沫，但由于它的每一个参与者的行为**看上去**都是理性的，没有人能够看出情况已经变得疯狂。[8] 跨国

29

投资流动（通过国际金融交易，比如贷款）更加剧"热"投资的需求，推动价格进一步上涨。尽管如此，各国央行等政府部门往往不愿干预，不愿"在盛宴进行的过程中拿走酒杯"，因为他们害怕公众会因为政府干预产生厌恶情绪。[9]

金德尔伯格写道："核心问题是中央银行能否抑制信贷供应的不稳定性，减缓投机活动，以避免危险的蔓延。"[10] 他怀疑央行是否"无所不知、无所不能"而足以做到这一点。有鉴于此，一个国际"最后贷款人"有助于减少这种危机的影响。当银行危机袭来、银行出乎意料地缺乏现金时，它们必须出售证券以筹集必要的资金。[11] 如果所有银行同时出售证券，而其他投资者也同样地"奔向出口"，由于价格已经崩溃，他们的资产也不会大幅升值。这些银行可能突然发现自己无力偿债（即无法履行其金融义务，例如偿还债务）。[12]

"最后贷款人"能做的就是向陷入困境的机构发放现金贷款，帮助他们渡过现金危机，要求他们在证券价格恢复时再清还贷款。这使整个经济体摆脱了一场更为严重的崩盘所带来的动荡和混乱。

语言表述

金德尔伯格把自己看作一个"文学经济学家"，他依赖于历史文本和叙事，在很大程度上以 18 世纪著名的哲学家和经济学家亚当·斯密*的风格为自己的原型。[13]

虽然金德尔伯格的写作中经常出现相当技术性的措辞，但《疯狂、惊恐和崩溃》中的技术材料却夹杂着精确而有趣的散文。它还以一种易读的历史趣闻语调为基础。例如，金德尔伯格指出，一些投资者无法抗拒在已知的资产泡沫上投资，价格持续上涨，他们确信自己会在崩溃来临之前卖出。为了说明这一点，他引用了一位在1720年著名的南海泡沫*上投资了500英镑（折算成现在的币值，大约是10万英镑或14万美元）的银行家的话，"当全世界都在疯狂时，我们必须在某种程度上模仿他们。"[14]（在南海泡沫期间，英国的南海公司获准与南美洲进行垄断贸易，股票上升到天文高度，然后急剧崩溃，破坏了整个英国经济。）他随后引用了当时美国跨国金融公司花旗集团的主席查克·普林斯*在2008年股市崩盘之前说过的话："只要音乐还在响着，你就得继续跳舞。"[15]

这幽默地表明，随着时间的流逝，金融界的这种行为是始终如一的。这些引用成对出现时带来的启示比单独出现时要大得多。它们一起可以直接支撑金德尔伯格的主要观点，即在经济史的疯狂、惊恐和崩溃中，存在着"生物规律性"。

---

1. 查尔斯·P. 金德尔伯格和罗伯特·Z. 阿利伯：《疯狂、惊恐和崩溃：金融危机史》，贝辛斯托克：帕尔格雷夫·麦克米伦出版社，2015年，第3页。
2. 金德尔伯格和阿利伯：《疯狂、惊恐和崩溃》，第3页。
3. 金德尔伯格和阿利伯：《疯狂、惊恐和崩溃》，第20页。
4. 金德尔伯格和阿利伯：《疯狂、惊恐和崩溃》，第52页。
5. 金德尔伯格和阿利伯：《疯狂、惊恐和崩溃》，第43页。
6. 金德尔伯格和阿利伯：《疯狂、惊恐和崩溃》，第43页。
7. 金德尔伯格和阿利伯：《疯狂、惊恐和崩溃》，第41页。
8. 金德尔伯格和阿利伯：《疯狂、惊恐和崩溃》，第63页。
9. 金德尔伯格和阿利伯：《疯狂、惊恐和崩溃》，第111页。
10. 金德尔伯格和阿利伯：《疯狂、惊恐和崩溃》，第101页。

11. 金德尔伯格和阿利伯:《疯狂、惊恐和崩溃》,第 281 页。

12. 金德尔伯格和阿利伯:《疯狂、惊恐和崩溃》,第 281 页。

13. 迈克尔·H.图尔克:《经济学建构中的历史观》,阿宾顿:劳特利奇出版社,
    2016 年,第 191 页。

14. 金德尔伯格和阿利伯:《疯狂、惊恐和崩溃》,第 57 页。

15. 金德尔伯格和阿利伯:《疯狂、惊恐和崩溃》,第 57 页。

6 思想支脉

要点 ⚷━━┥

- 金德尔伯格也关注金融危机是如何经常造成货币危机的；他还看到经济体内的"正反馈环"*——会自我放大的循环——使危机难以预防。

- 这些次要思想建立在金德尔伯格的主要观点之上，阐明了金融危机的复杂性。

- 货币危机强调了金融危机的国际层面，而"正反馈环"则揭示了金融危机的持久性。

其他思想

查尔斯·P. 金德尔伯格的《疯狂、惊恐和崩溃：金融危机史》的次要主题是金融危机和货币危机之间的关系，以及所谓的"正反馈环"。除了跨境投资流动增加，金德尔伯格还看到其他加剧全球经济不稳定的原因。其中之一是美国在 1971 年放弃了"金本位"*制度。[1]"金本位"是指一个国家将其货币价值与一定量的黄金直接挂钩的货币政策体系。1934 年，美国政府宣布一盎司黄金价值 35 美元，并将这个比例保持到 1971 年。

政府基于这种贵金属的固有价值发行货币有许多稳定的优点。其一是相对于其他货币，该货币价值不会过于动荡地升降（因为它与黄金挂钩，是"固定*的"）。当美元在 1971 年退出"金本位"时，它进入了一个"自由浮动"*的安排体系，在这种安排下，它的价值主要由国际货币市场和它们强烈的供求波动所决定。

其次，在金德尔伯格所考察的所有历史"狂热"中，20世纪80年代日本的资产泡沫*是最常被提及的。这个例子提出了"正反馈环"让繁荣与萧条的周期难以避免的深刻洞见：繁荣以一种无故障和不可抗拒的方式创造更多的繁荣，从而增强投资者和投机者的信心，而萧条则导致自我反噬的消极，使崩溃越来越糟。[2]

> "到1989年时，东京的闲聊是皇宫下面的土地市场价值比加利福尼亚所有房地产的市场价值还要高。"
> —— 查尔斯·P.金德尔伯格：《疯狂、惊恐和崩溃：金融危机史》

思想探究

由于过去几十年间美国在全球资本主义中的突出地位，美元的金本位制是整个全球体系稳定的支柱（"资本主义"在这里是指在世界范围内日益占主导地位的社会和经济体系，其中商业和投资是追求利润的行为）。其他国家可以将其货币与美元"挂钩"，不断重估本国货币以维持与美国的稳定汇率（美元本身被赋予黄金的稳定价值），这为全球提供了更加平稳的货币兑换。例如，1945年至1971年间运作的"布雷顿森林体系"*在美国、加拿大、西欧、澳大利亚和日本之间协调货币管理，它利用美国金本位政策的基石在这些国家之间创造稳定的汇率。

然而，当美国在1971年终止布雷顿森林体系时，这种稳定的动态彻底被打破了。美元进入"浮动汇率安排"，国际货币市场决定了它与其他货币相比的价值。国际货币投机者可能会在这样的市场中造成严重破坏：如果追求短期利润的人群情绪化地认定美元对英镑的价值变得越来越低，那么势头就会迅速发展，美元就会在国际市场上无理由地贬值，只因为由非理性投机者组成的"乌合之众"不想留下没人要的货币。[3] 金德尔伯格预测，美国脱离金本位，转向"浮动"货币安排，将成为金融不稳定性的新来源。[4]

在 20 世纪 80 年代后半期，日本货币和信贷供应的增长是极端的，包括全球投资的涌入，导致股票和房地产价格的飙升。[5] 日本银行广泛持有这两种资产，所以当股票和房地产价格上涨，这些银行的资本也相应增加。银行利用资本增加向投资股票或房地产的借款人提供更多贷款。以信贷的形式供应货币进一步提高这些资产的价格，反过来为这些贷款银行带来更大资本收益（来自他们持有资产的再次升值）。[6] 通过这个过程，"日本已经开发出了财经界的'永动机'。"银行借贷越多，他们看到自己的资产价格上涨越多，这给了他们更多的钱再次出借。[7]

自然地，当崩溃最终来临时，这种"永动机"将从相反方向影响市场。股票和房地产价格暴跌，导致银行的信用紧缩，进一步导致价格暴跌。[8] 日本的经济衰退严重而持久，从那以后，再没能见到任何类似高增长和繁荣的景象。

被忽视之处

虽然金德尔伯格对自由流动货币的危险提出了令人信服的理由，但我们也可认为这种安排实际上有某种平息"狂热"的益处。

像米尔顿·弗里德曼这样的经济学家认为控制一个国家货币供应量（流通中的货币量）是控制其经济表现的最佳工具。在经济过热时期，一个国家可以提高利率，使得借贷成本增加，从而缩减货币供应量，抑制过热（也许是狂热）的经济。在经济衰退时期，可以通过降低利率，让借贷成本更低，使得更多人愿意借钱来刺激经济（当他们花掉借来的钱时）。

但是，如果一个国家试图维持与其他国家的固定汇率（例如，将其货币与美元"挂钩"），则无法以这种方式增加或减少货币供应，因为这种举动将直接影响国际货币供应和需求。例如，如果阿根廷降低其利率，从而增加其货币供应，这也将增加阿根廷比索的国际供应，使得该货币变得不那么稀缺。在其他条件不变的情况下，阿根廷比索将会贬值——这是在汇率自由浮动时的结果，但不会是固定挂钩的结果。在固定汇率的体系中，阿根廷比索的特定挂钩价值必须通过国际协议来维持，这会阻止政府降低利率（即便有迫切的需要），因为此举将导致其货币脱离所协议好的固定国际价值。

因此，采取汇率自由浮动体系的国家可以通过利率调节而拥有控制自己货币供应的自由——没有义务在任何预定的挂钩水平上维持其货币的价值。在增长过速的过程中直接减少货币供应可以帮助减弱经济过热，因此自由浮动汇率实际上可以促进金融稳定。

---

1. 查尔斯·P. 金德尔伯格和罗伯特·Z. 阿利伯：《疯狂、惊恐和崩溃：金融危机史》，贝辛斯托克：帕尔格雷夫·麦克米伦出版社，2015年，第1页。
2. 金德尔伯格和阿利伯：《疯狂、惊恐和崩溃》，第206页。
3. 金德尔伯格和阿利伯：《疯狂、惊恐和崩溃》，第55—56页。
4. 金德尔伯格和阿利伯：《疯狂、惊恐和崩溃》，第1页。

5. 金德尔伯格和阿利伯：《疯狂、惊恐和崩溃》，第 207 页。

6. 金德尔伯格和阿利伯：《疯狂、惊恐和崩溃》，第 206 页。

7. 金德尔伯格和阿利伯：《疯狂、惊恐和崩溃》，第 207 页。

8. 金德尔伯格和阿利伯：《疯狂、惊恐和崩溃》，第 208 页。

7 历史成就

要点 🔑

- 《疯狂、惊恐和崩溃》被广泛认为是对金融危机的开拓性研究，并已成为经济学领域的经典之作。

- 《疯狂、惊恐和崩溃》是在一系列严重的金融危机之前出版的，显得有预言性，它为观察者提供了关于危机成因的、有说服力的解释。

- 金德尔伯格的论文驳斥了被称为货币主义的经济学理论，但也可以说，金德尔伯格可能没有充分考虑如何控制货币供应量才能稳定世界经济。

观点评价

查尔斯·P. 金德尔伯格的《疯狂、惊恐和崩溃：金融危机史》在 1978 年首版。公平地说，即使这本书借鉴了前辈经济学家海曼·明斯基的研究，金德尔伯格还是实现了他的雄心壮志，创作了他自己以国际视野研究金融灾难的经典著作。在整个过程中，他渊博的知识是显而易见的，无论是精心挑选的金融危机案例和当代名言的引用，还是他在描述繁荣和萧条的周期性阶段时呈现它们的方式。

随着全球经济日益相互依存，从金德尔伯格的"国际传播"*（或传染）的观点中，还有很多东西值得学习。据此观点，"金融危机经常从一个国家反弹到另一个国家。"[1] 这项突破性的观点从 1978 年以来有了越来越多的验证和引用；最近由欧盟资助的对金德尔伯格成就的一次广泛评估是其获得评论界认同进程中另一个值得注意的时刻。[2] 金德尔伯格的成功还在于他总是以引人入胜的写作方式表达他的想法，这为他赢得了"文学经济学家"的绰号。普林斯顿大学出版社的经济学编辑称他的书为"希望吸引更多读者的经济学家的典范"，这要归功于他精致而又平易近人的写作风格。[3]

自 1978 年以来，《疯狂、惊恐和崩溃》已经历了 7 个版本，每个版本都在前版的基础上更新，最近几版都是由罗伯特·Z.阿利伯编辑和更新。金德尔伯格在他的领域一直被誉为思想的巨人，该书仍然被投资者、学者、政治家和财经记者反复引用。例如，英国报纸《金融时报》在金德尔伯格 2003 年去世约 10 年后称他为"金融危机领域杰出的历史学家"。[4] 经济学家约翰·莫德林*和乔纳森·泰珀*合著的财经畅销书《红色密码：如何保护你的储蓄免受即将到来的危机》（2013）中将金德尔伯格的经典著作称为"泡沫圣经"。[5]

> "更多的疯狂、惊恐和崩溃可能会困扰我们，但本书的读者至少可以有预防免疫的能力。"
>
> —— 罗伯特·M.索洛：《疯狂、惊恐和崩溃：金融危机史》序言

当代成就

毫无疑问，《疯狂、惊恐和崩溃》取得的巨大成功部分归功于时机。当第 1 版于 1978 年出版时，一些经济史上最大的泡沫和崩溃即将发生。整个 20 世纪 70 年代，国际银行向墨西哥、巴西、阿根廷和其他 10 个发展中国家（"发展"在这里指的是他们的经济繁荣的程度相对比"发达"国家，如美国和德国落后）的政府和政府

所有企业提供贷款（即信贷）激增。[6] 这些国家的外债年增长率高达 20%，到 1982 年，他们的违约债务高达 8 000 亿美元。[7] 这就引燃了各个国家的金融危机和那些借贷给他们的国际银行的危机。正如黎巴嫩裔美国作家和投资者纳西姆·尼古拉斯·塔勒布 * 在他的《黑天鹅》（2007）中所记述的那样："在 1982 夏天，大型美国银行失去了它们过去所有的（累计）收益，几乎是它们在美国银行业历史上所赚到的一切"，都因为这个意外的违约 * 潮。[8]

在世界其他地方全球危机接踵而至，包括日本股市和房地产泡沫（1985—1989）*、东亚危机 *（1997）、科技公司繁荣而导致的美国股市互联网泡沫 *（1995—1999），以及美国、英国、西班牙、爱尔兰和冰岛的房地产泡沫（2002—2007）。每一次危机都是由信贷的急剧飙升引发的，正如《疯狂、惊恐和崩溃》2015 版所指出的，这些"信贷供应的激增似乎势不可挡"。[9]

在这麻烦不断的几十年间，金德尔伯格和海曼·明斯基的作品得到了更多的关注。金德尔伯格的书在金融群体的眼中越来越重要，而每个后续的版本都以更急切、更新近的材料来补充分析和消化，精益求精。[10]

局限性

如果说《疯狂、惊恐和崩溃》有一个主要局限，那就是它缺乏如何预防未来金融危机的思想。金德尔伯格在驳斥针对无节制放贷行为的流行补救措施方面很有说服力，例如，他否认增加监管是解决问题的答案。同他论点的其他方面一样，这种立场植根于历史证据；他提醒读者，"虽然银行监管已有 300 多年的历史，但对于银行倒闭或濒临倒闭的普遍反应是，需要更多的监管或更有效的监管。"[11] 他的立场还基于这样的观点，即因为狂热是由信贷的过度快速增长造成的，所以没有适合于解决这个问题的监管；[12] 这种周期性狂热与依赖于信贷而运行的资本主义实践密切相关。任何通过限制信贷来调节经济的尝试都会使整个系统陷入永久性衰退。

这个论点中有明显的失败主义倾向。并非所有的监管都是相同的，尽管新时代可能会带来新的问题，但它也可以提供新的解决方案。诺贝尔经济学奖得主保罗·克鲁格曼*驳斥了金德尔伯格对监管的态度，认为美国大萧条后的新银行监管制度为美国提供了"一个可行的解决方案，既包括担保又包括监督"，并提供了半个世纪的金融稳定期。[13] 克鲁格曼积极地辩说，这种治理可以更新并适应今天的需要，而金德尔伯格的书却一味地接受无节制的行为。金德尔伯格可能热衷于需要一个"最后贷款人"来拯救一个国家，使其免于金融危机（防止坏局面变成一场全面的全球灾难），但他似乎已经屈服于这样的信念，即严重的经济危机是资本主义系统不可避免的方面。

1. 查尔斯·P.金德尔伯格和罗伯特·Z.阿利伯：《疯狂、惊恐和崩溃：金融危机史》，贝辛斯托克：帕尔格雷夫·麦克米伦出版社，2015年，第185页。

2. 皮耶罗·帕索蒂和亚历山德罗·维切利："金德尔伯格与金融危机"，《金融化、经济、社会和可持续发展工作论文集》第104卷，2015年2月，登录日期2016年3月22日，http://fessud.eu/wp-content/uploads/2015/01/Kindleberger-and-Financial-Crises-Fessud-final_Working-Paper-104.pdf。

3. 《经济学人》："谈疯狂、惊恐和崩溃"，2003年7月19日，登录日期2016年3

月 22 日，http://www.economist.com/node/1923462。

4. 阿肖卡·莫迪："德国必须为修复银行业做出表率"，《金融时报》，2013 年 5 月 27 日，登录日期 2016 年 3 月 22 日，http://www.ft.com/intl/cms/s/0/10e7ccbe-c46f-11e2-9ac0-00144feab7de.html#axzz43Y4Huy4b。

5. 约翰·莫德林和乔纳森·泰珀：《红色密码：如何保护你的储蓄免受即将到来的危机》，霍博肯：约翰·威利父子出版公司，2013 年，第 193 页。

6. 金德尔伯格和阿利伯：《疯狂、惊恐和崩溃》，第 1 页。

7. 金德尔伯格和阿利伯：《疯狂、惊恐和崩溃》，第 5 页。

8. 纳西姆·尼古拉斯·塔勒布：《黑天鹅：如何应对不可预知的未来》，伦敦：企鹅出版社，2007 年，第 43 页。

9. 金德尔伯格和阿利伯：《疯狂、惊恐和崩溃》，第 16 页。

10. 金德尔伯格持久影响力的两个例子：《经济学人》，"谈疯狂、惊恐和崩溃"；以及保罗·克鲁格曼："中国抓住了机会"，《纽约时报》，2015 年 8 月 12 日，登录日期 2016 年 3 月 22 日，http://krugman.blogs.nytimes.com/2015/08/12/china-bites-the-cherry/?_r=0。

11. 金德尔伯格和阿利伯：《疯狂、惊恐和崩溃》，第 239 页。

12. 金德尔伯格和阿利伯：《疯狂、惊恐和崩溃》，第 239 页。

13. 保罗·克鲁格曼："我们为何监管"，《纽约时报》，2012 年 5 月 13 日，登录日期 2016 年 3 月 22 日，http://www.nytimes.com/2012/05/14/opinion/krugman-why-we-regulate.html。

8 著作地位

要点 ⚷━

- 金德尔伯格的著作显示了他长期以明确的国际视角研究金融危机的历史。

- 他在 1973 年出版的《大萧条的世界，1929—1939》比《疯狂、惊恐和崩溃》早了 5 年，并为他在后书中提出的论点奠定了基础。

- 虽然金德尔伯格已经是备受尊崇的经济学家，《疯狂、惊恐和崩溃》还是巩固了他的声誉和长远的影响。

定位

查尔斯·P. 金德尔伯格的《疯狂、惊恐和崩溃：金融危机史》可能直接建立在美国经济学家海曼·明斯基的思想基础之上，但它也推进了作者本人早期的研究。

1973 年，金德尔伯格出版了《大萧条的世界，1929—1939》，该书认为，20 世纪 30 年代的大萧条是广泛、深刻和长期的经济衰退，因为没有国际上的"最后贷款人"来拯救陷入困境而面临倒闭的银行等金融机构。[1] 这本书因偏离了该主题中以美国为中心的主流观点而显得激进。正如其他经济学家指出的那样，"早期的文献大多是美国人写的，主要关注美国的大萧条，而金德尔伯格则强调大萧条有一个突出的国际特点，尤其是欧洲层面的影响。"[2]

金德尔伯格认为，"最后贷款人"可以平息导致大萧条的恐慌和崩溃，但世界正处在一个尴尬的十字路口。第一次世界大战（1914—1918）后，作为世界经济前任领头羊的英国太疲弱而无法履行这一职责，而正在崛起的世界新领头羊美国不愿承担这种责任。[3] 因此，全球崩溃的"负反馈环"*（一种恶性循环）被触发，局面越来越糟，但没有"最后贷款人"来给这趟马上要失事的经济列车踩上刹车。

金德尔伯格认为，20 世纪 30 年代美国的领导力缺失与 20 世纪 70 年代的情况几乎如出一辙，当时"金本位"和布雷顿森林体系的崩溃导致全球经济系统摇摇欲坠。在金德尔伯格看来，这两个机制为全球经济提供了必需的稳定性保障——但在 1971 年，美国放弃了金本位，这又导致布雷顿森林外汇体系的废弃。对金德尔伯格来说，这就播下了未来不稳定的种子。[4] 鉴于随后的金融危机，认为他是对的合情合理。

> "金德尔伯格的论点来自他对大萧条的解读。"
>
> —— 罗伯特·斯基德尔斯基勋爵：
> 《疯狂、惊恐和崩溃：金融危机史》后记

整合

金德尔伯格杰出的职业生涯始于对外汇的兴趣。他的第一本书《国际短期资本流动》（1937）研究了资本（金融资源）是如何被投机者转移到世界各地来赚取更高利率的。该书还探讨了国际收支*变化（一个国家是世界其他地区的"债权人"还是"债务人"）所累积的国际债务。[5]《美元短缺》（1950）探讨了国家经济发展水平与其国际收支之间的关系。[6]

早期对国际贸易的关注或许可以解释金德尔伯格在《大萧条的世界，1929—1939》和《疯狂、惊恐和崩溃》中展现的独特的国际

视角。从这个意义上说，他对国际资本流动和国际收支的关注在他
的整个职业生涯中始终如一，稳步扩展到更广泛的经济和金融历史
视野。到 20 世纪 70 年代，金德尔伯格开始关注过去和现在的金融
危机的本质，特别关注恐慌与蔓延，以及对国际"最后贷款人"的
需求。

意义

《疯狂、惊恐和崩溃》对金德尔伯格的事业和思想传承非常重
要。他是麻省理工学院受人尊敬的经济学教授，由于他早前的作品
和出版物，尤其是《大萧条的世界，1929—1939》，他的名声已经
很稳固了。受加拿大著名经济学家约翰·肯尼斯·加尔布雷斯 * 的
称赞，这本书本身就是一部经典。[7]

随着《疯狂、惊恐和崩溃》的成功，金德尔伯格被认为是他的
领域的开创者。1978 年，他宣布，由于美国金本位和国际布雷顿
森林体系的崩溃，新的全球经济更加脆弱。此时正当 20 世纪 70 年
代末和 20 世纪 80 年代初，这种脆弱性开始全面影响全球经济，并
将持续 30 年以上。在 1982 到 2007 年间，全球经济经历了金融历
史上 10 次最大的金融泡沫中的 6 次。[8]金德尔伯格的书为分析这些
危机的根源"铺平了道路"，并考虑可以采取什么措施来最小化它
们对全球经济系统的影响。[9]他的这本书可以与《大萧条的世界》
的成就和流行度相匹敌，甚至有所超越，尽管毫无疑问，它是早期
研究中的思想的持续探索与延伸。

1. 查尔斯·P.金德尔伯格和罗伯特·Z.阿利伯:《疯狂、惊恐和崩溃:金融危机史》,贝辛斯托克:帕尔格雷夫·麦克米伦出版社,2015年,第185页。

2. 皮耶罗·帕索蒂和亚历山德罗·维切利:"金德尔伯格与金融危机",《金融化、经济、社会和可持续发展工作论文集》第104卷,2015年2月,登录日期2016年3月22日,http://fessud.eu/wp-content/uploads/2015/01/Kindleberger-and-Financial-Crises-Fessud-final_Working-Paper-104.pdf,第6页。

3. 查尔斯·P.金德尔伯格:《大萧条的世界,1929—1939》,伯克利、洛杉矶:加利福尼亚大学出版社,1973年,第292页。

4. 金德尔伯格:《大萧条的世界》,第308页。

5. 查尔斯·P.金德尔伯格:《国际短期资本流动》,纽约:哥伦比亚大学出版社,1937年。

6. 查尔斯·P.金德尔伯格:《美元短缺》,纽约:约翰·威利父子出版公司,1950年。

7. 金德尔伯格:《大萧条的世界,1929—1939》,第1页。

8. 金德尔伯格和阿利伯:《疯狂、惊恐和崩溃》,第18页。

9. 萨基斯·耶卡斯:"'差'而不同",《都柏林书评》第16卷,2010年冬季刊,登录日期2016年3月22日,http://www.drb.ie/essays/different-because-worse。

第三部分：学术影响

9 最初反响

要点 ⚷⊶

- 当金德尔伯格提出给大型金融机构提供救助的国际"最后贷款人"的概念时，他没有具体说明这个机构在现实中应该如何运作。

- 随后的金融危机证明这样一种"最后贷款人"确实是必要的，这些事件也被纳入《疯狂、惊恐和崩溃》的新版本中。

- 考虑到《疯狂、惊恐和崩溃》出版后世界经济变得越来越动荡，有更多人开始相信金德尔伯格所论述的非理性投资行为。

批评

1978 年一经出版，《疯狂、惊恐和崩溃：金融危机史》便大体上得到了同行的一致赞扬，虽然一些缺陷也被指出。《经济史评论》在 1979 年出版的一期中称赞了查尔斯·金德尔伯格为这样一个"显然处于蛮荒"的主题带来的"巨大的智识力量"，并说它产生了新的见解。[1] 但该评论也质疑了书中的结论，批评金德尔伯格强调需要一个国际"最后贷款人"，而没有解释这应该采取什么形式。[2]

《经济学杂志》还盛赞金德尔伯格在学术性和个人风格之间取得的平衡，但却质疑他的基本假设，即狂热的"亢奋"时期反映了投资者和机构的"非理性"行为。[3] 这篇早期的评论认为这种行为与市场效率是可以相容的，因此站在了当时流行的有效市场假设理论这一边（与金德尔伯格的观点相背）。[4] 这位评论者还认为金德尔伯格对"最后贷款人"的热情是"模糊的"，并贬低了所谓的"文学经济学"，也即作品平易近人的叙事写作风格。[5]

"金德尔伯格关于最后贷款人的热情显得有些含糊。"
—— 帕特里克·闵福德："查尔斯·P. 金德尔伯格的
《疯狂、惊恐和崩溃：金融危机史》",《经济学杂志》

回应

当金德尔伯格写出《疯狂、惊恐和崩溃》时，学术环境在很大程度上忠于有效市场假说的理论及其投资者行为趋于理性的假设。基于金德尔伯格的观察，事实上这远非理性，他对自己所在领域的主流观点提出了重大挑战。他坚持自己的论点，并在后续修订版本中贯彻始终，最终评论家们理解了这个结论。

《疯狂、惊恐和崩溃》首版的评论者注意到，金德尔伯格关于过往金融危机的许多例子来自 1719—1929 年期间，"也涉及一些最近的事件"。[6] 然而，伴随着 1982 年的金融危机*，宏观经济进入了新一轮的动荡和脆弱期。金德尔伯格和他在 2003 年去世之后的继任者罗伯特·Z. 阿利伯从 1989 年到 2015 年间以 6 个新版本的《疯狂、惊恐和崩溃》对此作出回应。每一版都有大量的新材料来进行研究、分析和比较。例如，1996 版包括了对 1987 年美国股市崩盘*的分析（"黑色星期一"，因为美国和伊朗的短暂冲突，市场情绪紧张导致股票价格暴跌）和对 1995 年比索贬值*的分析（墨西哥政府决定将比索对美元汇率降低 15%，投资者试图出售他们在墨西哥的投资，其结果是危机蔓延到亚洲市场）。2000 年版包括了对 1997 年开始于泰国、并迅速蔓延到其他东亚国家的东亚金融危机的研究。没有一个新案例研究是孤立的，它们都成为关于金融危机、它们共有的"生物规律性"（一系列持续一致的发展阶段）以及如何应对危机的庞大论述的一部分。

不久之后，金德尔伯格关于国际"最后贷款人"的提议也获得了更多的支持。政治学家罗伯特·基欧汉 * 发展了这个理论，并将其重新命名为"霸权 * 稳定理论"，此乃久而久之的一个政治学标签[7]（"霸权"在这里指的是一个政治或经济超级大国的领导地位）。基欧汉自己注意到了关于这个话题日益增长的文献资料，并在他的著作《霸权之后：世界政治经济中的合作与纷争》（1984）中对其进行了详细的探讨。[8] 一场新的对话就此开始。

冲突与共识

随着时间的推移，《疯狂、惊恐和崩溃》被大多数学术和金融群体视为"经典"。[9] 然而，即使在尊崇金德尔伯格的研究时，这些批评者仍然对其中心内容存有一些疑问，例如他对"金融危机"不确切的定义。[10] 虽然金德尔伯格自己已经承认这个关键词语无法被任何措辞精确定义并获得一致认可，但批评者还是坚持明确定义的必要性。[11] 同样，书中较少区分引起大萧条的危机和并未引发大萧条的危机。[12]

除了对本书实际内容的争议之外，还存在广泛的理论挑战。有效市场假设理论并没有走远，该理论的著名宣讲者、经济学家和作家伯顿·G.马尔基尔 * 在他最近出版的畅销书《漫步华尔街》（其最新版本也于 2015 年出版）中还在颂扬它的优点。在马尔基尔看来，一个"狂热"投资者迟早会意识到他们资产的真正价值，并采取相应的行动，也即理性的行动。"虽然短期内的股票市场可能是投票机制，从长远来看，它是一种称量机制，真正的价值最终会得到体现。"[13] 金德尔伯格和他的继任者阿利伯不会给有效市场假设理论任何机会，阿利伯的 2015 年新版这样说：有效市场假设理论以为投资者有"千里眼"。[14]

1. W. 阿什沃思："评查尔斯·P. 金德尔伯格《疯狂、惊恐和崩溃：金融危机史》"，《经济史评论》第 32 卷，1979 年第 3 期，第 421—422 页。

2. 阿什沃思："《疯狂、惊恐和崩溃》"，第 422 页。

3. 帕特里克·闵福德："评查尔斯·P. 金德尔伯格《疯狂、惊恐和崩溃：金融危机史》"，《经济学杂志》第 89 卷，1979 年 12 月，第 947 页。

4. 闵福德："《疯狂、惊恐和崩溃》"，第 947 页。

5. 闵福德："《疯狂、惊恐和崩溃》"，第 947、948 页。

6. 阿什沃思："《疯狂、惊恐和崩溃》"，第 421 页。

7. 斯蒂芬·梅尔顿："谈金德尔伯格与霸权：从柏林到麻省理工及其归程"，鲍登数字共享，2013 年 9 月 29 日，登录日期 2016 年 3 月 22 日，http://digitalcommons.bowdoin.edu/cgi/viewcontent.cgi?article=1003&context=econpapers。

8. 梅尔顿："谈金德尔伯格与霸权"。

9. 参见克里斯托弗·科布拉克和米拉·威尔金斯：《历史与金融危机：20 世纪的教训》，纽约：劳特利奇出版社，2013 年，第 3 页。金融圈内的例子可参见贾森·茨威格："读完便是丰收：投资者的最佳书目"，《华尔街日报》，2014 年 11 月 28 日，登录日期 2016 年 3 月 22 日，http://www.wsj.com/articles/read-it-and-reap-the-best-books-for-investors-1417213387。

10. 科布拉克和威尔金斯：《历史与金融危机》，第 3 页。

11. 科布拉克和威尔金斯：《历史与金融危机》，第 4 页。

12. 理查德·西勒："金融动荡与萧条：经济史视角"，社会科学研究网：列维经济研究所工作论文第 47 卷，1991 年 4 月，第 3 页。

13. 伯顿·G. 马尔基尔："有效市场假说及其批评"，《经济学视角期刊》第 17 卷，2003 年第 1 期，第 61 页。

14. 查尔斯·P. 金德尔伯格和罗伯特·Z. 阿利伯：《疯狂、惊恐和崩溃：金融危机史》，贝辛斯托克：帕尔格雷夫·麦克米伦出版社，2015 年，第 53—56 页。

10 后续争议

要点 ⚙━┥

- 随着金融危机*的持续加深，金德尔伯格的思想受到更加认真的对待，尤其是建立一个能够救助那些深陷困境的大型金融机构的国际"最后贷款人"的提议。

- 建立在单一国家领导地位基础上的"霸权稳定"理论逐渐演变为对"最后贷款人"具体情况的清晰描述。

- 自《疯狂、惊恐和崩溃》出版以来，经济学学科已经通过行为经济学等新领域对非理性投资行为进行了研究，它借鉴了心理学领域，通过研究心理和行为来解释经济决策。

应用与问题

查尔斯·P. 金德伯格在《疯狂、惊恐和崩溃：金融危机史》中关于金融危机的观点是提议在全球范围内进行认真的政策协调。即便如此，他对国际"最后贷款人"在现实中的愿景看上去还是有些模糊，正如评论者所指出的那般。

从 20 世纪 80 年代开始，经济学家和政治学家受金德尔伯格思想的启发，开始面对设计这样一个实体的挑战。美国政治学家罗伯特·基欧汉在《霸权之后：世界政治经济中的合作与纷争》（1984）一书中开始设想一个现实场景中的国际"最后贷款人"。[1] 杰出的经济学家巴里·艾肯格林*在 1987 年写了《国际货币体系的霸权稳定理论》一文，其中他研究了实现国际货币协调所必需的条件、制度和领导力程度。[2] 这个问题让艾肯格林保持了长期的研究兴趣。

国际经济关系学者罗伯特·吉尔平*受金德尔伯格立场的影响，出版了《国际关系的政治经济学》（1987）。该书考察了二战后美国在全球金融结构中的领导地位及其是如何衰落的。吉尔平认为，美国在创造国际金融合作中占据绝对主导地位。[3] 这些以及其他许多受金德尔伯格启发的研究，表明了他的洞见是如何被运用的。受金德尔伯格影响的思想家认识到金融危机本质上是国际性的，并倾向于得出稳定金融危机需要新的国际合作的结论。实现这一目标是一个持续的挑战——也许在当前经济民族主义*日益发展的时代变得更加困难，经济民族主义认为一个国家以自己的经济健康为完全的、毫无妥协的、至高无上的导向，可以牺牲全球经济的整体健康为代价。

> "过去十年来的金融创新大大提高了美国金融体系整体的稳定性和韧性，但这些改进不太可能终结查尔斯·金德尔伯格所谓的疯狂和惊恐。"
>
> —— 蒂莫西·F.盖特纳："美国金融体系面临的变化和挑战"，《国际清算银行评论》

思想流派

《疯狂、惊恐和崩溃》最早发表于有效市场假说理论的鼎盛时期，其假设是投资者的行为是理性的。与主流思维方式不同，这本书在思考导致灾难性危机的经济周期本质上另辟蹊径。从1982年开始，世界经历了一系列金融危机，金德尔伯格的作品突然变得引人注目：对泡沫以及非理性的投资行为的新认识改变了人们头脑中既定的思维方式。[4] 举个例子，行为经济学是这个时期出现的一个快速发展的领域，它认为投资者通常远离理性，而且反映了诸如过度自信、偏见判断和羊群心理等心理偏见。像金德尔伯格一样，行为经济学家相信（和担心）这样的行为会使泡沫自我应验，也就是说，当每个人都认为资产价格会上涨时，他们就会购买资产，从而导致价格上涨；当所有人都认为价格会下跌时，他们就会抛售资产，导致价格暴跌。[5]

学者们在探索国际"最后贷款人"如何在政治上运作时形成了一个更广泛的思想学派。更多致力于制定现实危机处理策略的政治家也参与到这场持续的学术辩论中。例如，美国前财政部长蒂莫西·盖特纳*在他回忆 2004 年对投资银行过于自满的警告时，就引用了《疯狂、惊恐和崩溃》中的话，并说该书深深影响了他本人对金融危机的看法。[6]

当代研究

自从 2003 年金德尔伯格去世以后，经济学家罗伯特·Z. 阿利伯持续编辑并更新随后的《疯狂、惊恐和崩溃》。他担当起该书项目持续发展的主人角色，在它业已庞大的全景中持续增添金融危机和非理性行为的新例子。

在最新的第 7 版中，阿利伯以自己的新创见把该书的论点再推进一步。他研究了过去 40 年间一系列持续发生的金融危机案例——首先是发生在 20 世纪 80 年代早期的墨西哥和南美的金融危机，紧接着是 1990 年的日本经济崩溃，然后是 1997 年的东亚金融危机，最后是 2007 和 2008 年影响数个国家的房地产市场崩溃。他认为，这些"一波又一波的"由信贷推动的繁荣和萧条是因果相关的。[7]当导致一个国家狂热的国际货币突然逃离这个国家并引起恐慌时，这些货币的大部分被转移到另一个国际地点，开始激发另一场（病态的）繁荣。[8]阿利伯认为，大致同一批在世界各地流溢并受大型全球银行引导的国际货币是这些繁荣及后续萧条的背后推手。这是大胆有力且高度确切的论点，与金德尔伯格的原著精神交相辉映。

除了阿利伯对金德尔伯格论点的学术发展之外，全球学术界、金融界、政治界和新闻界都在广泛地讨论它。这本著作在商业世界也大受欢迎。一个私人商业咨询集团甚至在其官网上介绍这本书，宣称它应该是"从中央银行的主管到普通银行家，从投资者到普通商业人士，从政府大厅到普通起居室，所有人的必读书"。[9]金德尔伯格的思想现在被多个领域广泛接受，其精确性与远见卓识在世界各地被持续关注，声名远扬。

1. 罗伯特·基欧汉：《霸权之后：世界政治经济中的合作与纷争》，普林斯顿：普林斯顿大学出版社，1984 年。

2. 巴里·艾肯格林："国际货币体系的霸权稳定理论"，载《各国能否达成一致？国际经济合作中的问题》，理查德·库珀等编，华盛顿特区：布鲁金斯学会，1989 年，第 255—298 页。

3. 罗伯特·吉尔平：《国际关系的政治经济学》，普林斯顿：普林斯顿大学出版社，1987 年。

4. 《经济学人》，"谈疯狂、惊恐和崩溃"，2003 年 7 月 19 日，登录日期 2016 年 3 月 22 日，http://www.economist.com/node/1923462。

5. 托德·A.努普：《商业周期经济学：理解从繁荣到萧条的衰退和低迷》，加利福尼亚州圣芭芭拉：普雷格出版社，2015 年，第 172 页。

6. 蒂莫西·F.盖特纳：《压力测试：金融危机之反思》，纽约：皇冠出版社，2014 年。

7. 查尔斯·P.金德尔伯格和罗伯特·Z.阿利伯：《疯狂、惊恐和崩溃：金融危机史》，贝辛斯托克：帕尔格雷夫·麦克米伦出版社，2015 年，第 ix 页。

8. 金德尔伯格和阿利伯：《疯狂、惊恐和崩溃》，第 ix 页。

9. 盖尔·弗斯勒："金德尔伯格的金融危机课"，盖尔·弗斯勒集团，2013 年 4 月 28 日，登录日期 2016 年 3 月 22 日，http://www.gailfosler.com/lessons-from-kindleberger-on-the-financial-crisis。

11 当代印迹

要点 🔑

- 《疯狂、惊恐和崩溃》仍然是经济学领域流行的经典著作。

- 关于如何遏制金融危机的问题仍然是当今经济学家和政策制定者面临的挑战。

- 采取固定汇率制能否部分解决问题仍然是一个有争议的话题。

地位

查尔斯·P. 金德尔伯格的《疯狂、惊恐和崩溃：金融危机史》在 1978 年首次出版后 40 多年仍然具有影响力和重要性。谈到当下事件，这本书也被经常提及，例如，当中国股市在 2015 年夏天崩盘时，英国经济杂志《经济学人》在这则新闻上开辟了一个与金德尔伯格框架直接相关的专题："伟大的查尔斯·金德尔伯格在他的著作《疯狂、惊恐和崩溃》中描述了泡沫形成和破裂的模式。"[1]

金德尔伯格的提议已经影响到政治经济的最高层面。美国经济学家罗伯特·M. 索洛在《疯狂、惊恐和崩溃》的前言中说，金德尔伯格"肯定会着迷，或许会感到欣慰，如果他看到 2008 年金融危机期间，美联储不仅作为银行系统的最后贷款人，而且几乎成为整个经济体的最后贷款人"。[2] 此外，在金德尔伯格早期著作《大萧条的世界，1929—1939》40 周年纪念版中，编辑们注意到在全球金融危机和美国政治功能失调时期，他的"霸权稳定理论"尤显重要。[3] 这本书的出版简介突出了该书在全球经济政治中的重要角色：

"这本经济史上的杰作揭示了为什么美国财政部长劳伦斯·萨默斯*会在 2008 年全球金融危机最黑暗的时刻，转向金德尔伯格和他的同僚寻求指导。"[4]

> "查尔斯·金德尔伯格权威性的《疯狂、惊恐和崩溃》无疑是这个领域最严谨、也是最伟大的著作。"
>
> —— 尼克·默里："金融荒唐事大赏"，《财务顾问》

互动

　　各国仍然可以选择固定汇率的或自由浮动汇率的货币政策。虽然金德尔伯格认为固定汇率更加稳定，但国际货币基金组织*的研究却严重挑战了这一点，该研究显示这两个体系之间的波动性没有太大差别。[5] 国际货币基金组织是为确保国际金融稳定与合作而设立的机构；它通常给处于金融困境的国家提供贷款，以实现其经济的结构性改变，如实施削减开支或国有企业的私有化。

　　关于谁应该为 2008 年金融危机负责的争论还在继续。纽约的投资银行雷曼兄弟*在 2008 年破产，成了这场危机的替罪羊。金德尔伯格将会把雷曼兄弟看作更大经济动态背景下的一个小角色：在此背景中信贷供应全面飙升，投资者们正进入一个非理性乐观预测的"亢奋"阶段。[6]

　　更普遍地说，《疯狂、惊恐和崩溃》的基本观点是金融危机具有贯穿整个历史的"生物规律性"，信贷供应过剩是首要问题——此观点遭到大量分析 2008 年金融危机的研究者的反对。他们中的许多人认为，这次金融危机的成因在当时背景下是完全独特的，与历史上的其他金融危机没有什么共同之处。

持续争议

在他职业生涯后期，金德尔伯格坚持认为，20 世纪 70 年代美国放弃金本位、原布雷顿森林体系的国家之间的金融关系终结，以及美元和许多其他国家货币转向自由浮动利率机制正成为全球经济不稳定性的新来源。国际货币基金组织 2004 年的一份报告直接挑战了这个观点。研究发现，在过去 30 年中，固定汇率与浮动汇率的波动大致相同——这是可能的，因为与美元挂钩的货币仍必须随着美元对世界其他货币（非挂钩）汇率的变化而上下浮动。[7] 此研究还显示，汇率自由浮动对某个国家的国际贸易进出影响很小，[8] 这意味着固定汇率体系可能并没有带来金德尔伯格所预见的稳定性。

许多杰出的评论家和作家在分析 2008 的崩溃时忽略了金德尔伯格的洞察力。雷曼兄弟仍然经常被认为是危机的根源，这体现在一些已出版畅销书的标题中：由雷曼兄弟前副董事长劳伦斯·G.麦克唐纳 * 和经济学家帕特里克·罗宾逊写的《常识的溃败：雷曼兄弟破产内幕》（2009），以及财经记者维琪·沃德 * 写的《魔鬼赌场：雷曼兄弟内部的友谊、背叛与豪赌》（2010）。[9]

还有一些评论家认为 2008 年金融危机是完全独特的，界定了其他一些因素为导致危机的"真正"原因。财经记者斯科特·帕特森的《宽客》（2010）一书认为，极具数学思维的华尔街"定量分析师们"在金融危机爆发前一年接管了金融体系的大部分，他们应该对此负责。[10] 当时的一位交易员大胆地出版了《我是如何引发信贷危机的》（2009）一书，表示他独自为此事件负责。[11] 这些书都没有从金德尔伯格更广泛、更具历史意义的视角来看待这次金融危机。

1. 梧桐树专栏："中国股市：大跃退"，《经济学人》，2015年7月8日，登录日期2016年3月22日，http://www.economist.com/blogs/buttonwood/2015/07/chinas-stockmarket。

2. 查尔斯·P.金德尔伯格和罗伯特·Z.阿利伯：《疯狂、惊恐和崩溃：金融危机史》，贝辛斯托克：帕尔格雷夫·麦克米伦出版社，2015年，第viii页。

3. 查尔斯·P.金德尔伯格：《大萧条的世界，1929—1939》，J.布拉德福德·德隆和巴里·艾肯格林编，洛杉矶、伯克利：加利福尼亚大学出版社，2013年，第ix页。

4. 加里福利亚大学出版社："《大萧条的世界，1929—1939》"，登录日期2016年3月22日，http://www.ucpress.edu/book.php?isbn=9780520275850。

5. 彼得·克拉克等："汇率波动与贸易流动——一些新的证据"，国际货币基金组织，2004年5月，第54—55页，登录日期2016年3月21日，http://www.imf.org/external/np/res/exrate/2004/eng/051904.pdf。

6. 金德尔伯格和阿利伯：《疯狂、惊恐和崩溃》，第15页。

7. 克拉克等："汇率波动"，第54—55页。

8. 克拉克等："汇率波动"，第55页。

9. 劳伦斯·G.麦克唐纳和帕特里克·罗宾逊：《常识的溃败：雷曼兄弟破产内幕》，纽约：三河出版社，2009年；维琪·沃德：《魔鬼赌场：雷曼兄弟内部的友谊、背叛与豪赌》，霍布肯：约翰·威利父子出版公司，2010年。

10. 斯科特·帕特森：《宽客：看新生代数学高手如何征服并近乎摧毁华尔街》，纽约：皇冠出版社，2010年。

11. 哲弥石川：《我是如何引发信贷危机的：金融灾难内部人士的故事》，伦敦：圣像图书，2009年。

12 未来展望

要点 👈━┐

- 金德尔伯格的文本仍然是经济学家和政治家寻求稳定世界经济的试金石。

- 《疯狂、惊恐和崩溃》是与时俱进、不断发展的文本，它确切说明了金融危机的运作方式，并且为全球经济动荡提出了可能的解决方案。

- 《疯狂、惊恐和崩溃》以一种基于历史背景的、着眼当下的和人性化的方式解释了经济繁荣和萧条的周期循环。

潜力

在当今的时代背景下，查尔斯·P.金德尔伯格作品的重要性和影响力必将持续下去，尤其是因为当今的背景如此紧密（而且令人恐惧）地反映了《疯狂、惊恐和崩溃：金融危机史》在 20 世纪 70 年代所预示的担忧。例如，2015 年 6 月 12 日，中国股市崩盘，上海证交所股票交易市值下跌三分之一。[1] 经过一段时间的稳定后，同一市场在 2016 年初再次崩盘，并引发了全球股市回落。[2] 油价泡沫也同时爆发，给世界经济带来了巨大的通货紧缩压力——货币价值上升，物价下跌。

所有这些都是大新闻，而金德尔伯格的文章也被评论员频繁引用。关于中国 2015 年的股灾，香港大学两位有影响力的教授表示："尽管责备的游戏还在继续，但历史学家查尔斯·金德尔伯格 1978 年的著作《疯狂、惊恐和崩溃：金融危机史》完美地解释了中国正在经历什么。"[3]谈到油价暴跌,一位评论员写道:"能源周期符合金德尔伯格教授在他经典的金融史著作《疯狂、惊恐和崩溃》中描述的经典情景。"[4]在重大全球经济事件的对话中,金德尔伯格永远不会缺席,这些例子只是冰山一隅。甚至可以说,这本书会随着时间的推移而越来越重要。

> "中国的问题很像 20 世纪 90 年代初的日本,家庭储蓄的金额远远大于企业的可获利投资。"
>
> —— 罗伯特·Z. 阿利伯:《疯狂、惊恐和崩溃:金融危机史》

未来方向

自从金德尔伯格 2003 年去世以来,《疯狂、惊恐和崩溃》版本持续更新,其中包括许多新的材料和分析,以及持续演变的论点。此书现任的合著者兼编辑、芝加哥大学教授罗伯特·Z. 阿利伯在 2015 年新版中加了一个关于中国的后记,警告说其高增长率实际上是面临破灭风险的泡沫,尤其因为大部分增长都建立在信贷增长的基础上。2016 年初中国股市急剧下跌,导致全球股票抛售,这可被视为从金德尔伯格周期的"狂热"向"恐慌"阶段的转变。一位美国学者曾说,鉴于中国的这些事件,"第 8 版《疯狂、惊恐和崩溃》的需求很快就会显现出来了。"[5]阿利伯从金德尔伯格手中接过接力棒;在当今全球经济形势下,从 1978 年开始的关于《疯狂、惊恐和崩溃》的讨论变得越来越广泛,且越来越紧迫。

金德尔伯格缓和市场与经济动荡(不稳定)的核心建议是建立国际"最后贷款人"的机制。虽然金德尔伯格第一次提出建议时就存在一个全球性的金融机构,但他并不相信它能够充分地填补他界定的"机制真空"。国际货币基金组织成立于20世纪40年代，旨在充当这样一个国际"最后贷款人"。[6] 然而，许多经济学家质疑它的有效性，质疑"国际货币基金组织作为对金融危机国家提供该国货币的供应机构，是否激化了那些肆意挥霍的国家的财政政策"。[7]

最终，国际货币基金组织或其他任何形式的国际"最后贷款人"必须完成一项困难的平衡：它必须存在，并准备好在金融危机时提供贷款，但它又必须始终使提供这种帮助具有一定的不确定性，这样，它的存在才不会鼓励那种鲁莽的行为。[8] 在最新版的《疯狂、惊恐和崩溃》中有一页关于"国际货币基金组织作为国际最后贷款人的评估报告"，其中有一句颇具讽刺意味的判决："国际货币基金组织已经失去了管理国际货币体系的初衷"，并且没有充分认识到巨大的跨境投资流动对全球经济构成威胁。[9] 建立适当的"最后贷款人"看起来将是一项长期持续的工程。

小结

虽然大量借鉴了经济学家海曼·明斯基的观点，但金德尔伯格的《疯狂、惊恐和崩溃》确实是一项久经时间考验的、真正具有开创性的研究。甚至可以说，它已经与当今经济面临的最紧迫、最有风险的问题越来越相关。这本书出版于1978年，当时经济学系盛行市场理性和效率的数学模型。《疯狂、惊恐和崩溃》没有跟随这种趋势，而是提供了一个关于市场如何运作的新视角，一个被证明了具有预见性的观点。金德尔伯格使用了"文学经济学"那令人愉快的叙事风格论证了这样一个观点：不仅国际经济本身具有不稳定性（由信贷激增导致，正如明斯基之前在国内背景下所提出的那样），而且 20 世纪 70 年代美国抛弃金本位和布雷顿森林体系使得它更容易陷入危机。

金德尔伯格以一种创新的、非正统的方式审视经济史，其框架最终是对未来发展的预期。不仅如此，他还将这种从狂热到恐慌到崩溃的持续周期诊断为信贷激增（以及阿利伯后来增补并分析的跨国投资流动）的作用。这个结论仍然有争议，但金德尔伯格对这些周期各阶段详细和具有历史依据的描述，以令人信服的方式揭示了当今的全球经济事件——使实现国际经济稳定的雄心成为可能。在追求这一重要目标时，《疯狂、惊恐和崩溃》仍然是必不可少的读物。

---

1. 凯蒂·艾伦："中国股市为何深陷危机？"，《卫报》，2015 年 7 月 8 日，登录日期 2016 年 3 月 22 日，http://www.theguardian.com/business/2015/jul/08/china-stock-market-crisis-explained。

2. 威尔·赫顿："我们为何对全世界股市崩盘无能为力？"，《卫报》，2016 年 1 月 17 日，登录日期 3 月 22 日，http://www.theguardian.com/commentisfree/2016/jan/17/china-economic-crisis-world-economy-global-capitalism。

3. 沈联涛和肖耿："中国压力测试实况"，世界报业辛迪加：全球评论版，2015 年 7 月 21 日，登录日期 2016 年 3 月 22 日，http://www.project-syndicate.org/commentary/china-stock-market-government-intervention-by-andrew-sheng-and-xiao-geng-2015-07?barrier=true。

4. 迈克尔·莱维特："油价将再次下跌 50%"，迈克尔·莱维特教你稳赚不赔，2015 年 9 月 28 日，登录日期 2016 年 3 月 22 日，http://suremoneyinvestor.com/2015/09/oil-is-going-to-fall-by-50-again。

5. 约瑟夫·P.乔伊斯:"《疯狂、惊恐和崩溃》的持久价值",资本兴衰,2015年12月14日,登录日期2016年3月22日,http://blogs.wellesley.edu/jjoyce/2015/12/14/the-enduring-relevance-of-manias-panics-and-crashes-2/。

6. 查尔斯·P.金德尔伯格和罗伯特·Z.阿利伯:《疯狂、惊恐和崩溃:金融危机史》,贝辛斯托克:帕尔格雷夫·麦克米伦出版社,2015年,第35页。

7. 金德尔伯格和阿利伯:《疯狂、惊恐和崩溃》,第35页。

8. 金德尔伯格和阿利伯:《疯狂、惊恐和崩溃》,第35页。

9. 金德尔伯格和阿利伯:《疯狂、惊恐和崩溃》,第310—312页。

术语表

1. **资产**：某人或某物拥有的财力资源或财产，具备一定的经济价值。

2. **白芝浩原则**：在 1873 年出版的《伦巴第街》一书中，英国商人和作家白芝浩竭力主张英格兰银行应当以惩罚利率给那些处境堪忧但仍具有偿付能力的银行提供大量贷款，从而平息金融恐慌。这项政策广受各大中央银行的欢迎，后来被称作"白芝浩原则"。

3. **收支差额**：该术语用以表述一个国家与世界其他国家的借贷关系。

4. **行为经济学**：一个较新的经济学领域，研究个人和机构的决策过程，试图纠正"理性"行为的假设。市场参与者心理上的、情绪上的以及高度非理性层面上的因素在该领域得到强调。

5. **行为金融学**：一个金融学领域，探索市场参与者的心理特点以解释市场动向，特别是系统出现的非理性误差。

6. **生物规律性**：金德尔伯格使用的一个术语，认为金融危机有共同的发生阶段和繁荣萧条交替出现的底层动态。

7. **繁荣和萧条**：一个经济循环周期，先是经济快速增长趋向繁荣，随后是突如其来的经济崩盘。

8. **布雷顿森林体系**：战后大量欧洲国家达成的一项周密协议，在这些国家以及其他金融系统之间建立货币体系。它从 1945 年开始生效，直到 1971 年美国放弃金本位制度。

9. **泡沫**：当资产、证券或商品的价格以基本经济原则无法解释的方式大幅上涨时，泡沫就产生了。

10. **资本**：诸如现金或其他有价值资产的金融资源，对其所有者来说是现成可利用的。

11. **资本主义**：一种经济体制，生产资料被私人占有，并用于追求利润。商品和服务的生产以供求规律为基础。

12. **中央银行**：一个政府机构，为管控国家利率、货币供应和解决其他货币问题而设立。

13. **古典经济学**：18 世纪晚期和 19 世纪早期的思潮，主要倡导建立自由市场。

14. **传染**：指市场动荡的传播，不管是地区市场、国家市场还是国际市场。传染可以是跨越国界的经济繁荣，也可以是经济危机。

15. **信贷紧缩**：一种经济形势，贷款或其他形式的投资资本突然难以获得。

16. **跨境投资流**：跨越国界的金融安排，其典型形式是贷款、收购和信贷。

17. **货币危机**：由一国货币价值降低引发的危机，会造成该国货币对他国货币汇率的波动。这种贬值和不稳定性会使投资者望而却步，也使该国难以将汇率保持在固定水平。

18. **违约**：规定期限内未能偿还贷款或贷款的利息。

19. **通货紧缩**：货币价值增长，由此引发商品价格下降。

20. **移位**：当重大事件——比如战争或放松管制的新规实施——致使经济繁荣时，就产生了移位。有时新技术或新发明带来的市场盈利性激增也会带来冲击，比如 20 世纪 90 年代末期互联网发明之后的信息技术市场繁荣。

21. **互联网泡沫**：工业化国家在 20 世纪 90 年代末期所经历的股市价格巨幅增长，得益于科技公司的发展壮大。

22. **东亚危机**：1997 年始于泰国、并迅速蔓延到其他东亚国家的金融危机。

23. **经济史**：对过往经济现象的研究。

24. **经济民族主义**：一种意识形态，某个国家不顾世界经济的总体健康，而将本国经济的健康运转彻底且毫不妥协地放在首位。

25. **经济学**：一门试图描述有限资源在欲求无限的世界中的生产、分配和消费的社会科学。

26. **有效**：在经济学中，"有效"是一种所有资源都得到最佳配置的状态，也即它们能在最少浪费的同时发挥最大的作用。

27. **有效市场假说**：一种观点，认为包括股价在内的资产价格能充分体现有关该资产或企业的所有可用信息。

28. **联邦储备系统（美联储）**：美国的中央银行，负责调控国家的货币和金融体系。

29. **金融危机**：一个含义广泛的术语，描述金融资产或财产的价格急速、且大幅下降时的各种情形。

30. **1982 年金融危机**：一场持久的危机，原因是许多拉丁美洲国家无力承担外债，特别是美国银行的债务，这使危机蔓延海外。它始于1982 年夏天，当时墨西哥总理通知美联储该国将无法偿还其高达800 亿美元的外债。随后，其他南美国家纷纷效仿。

31. **2008 年金融危机**：自大萧条以来最严重的一次经济危机，突出特点是大范围的银行救助、股市崩盘和房地产市场破产。

32. **金融不稳定假说**：美国经济学家海曼·明斯基提出的观点，认为在信贷的刺激下，经济繁荣会导致鲁莽的投资行为。

33. **金融监管**：其典型是政府机关通过规定好的要求和指导方针对金融机构进行监督。

34. **固定汇率**：政府将该国货币的价值同其他国家货币或一篮子货币的价值相挂钩。有时也通过宣称货币等价于一定量的黄金而将其汇率固定。

35. **自由浮动汇率**：货币的汇率未被政府固定，而能在国际货币市场上波动。

36. **全球经济**：在贸易与产业中，世界各国的经济相互依存，形成一套经济体系。

37. **金本位**：一国政府宣布该国货币等价于一定量的黄金，从而将其货币价值固定。

38. **大萧条**：一场旷日持久的严重经济萧条，始于 1929 年，一直持续到第二次世界大战。

39. **霸权**：一个国家突出的领导地位，或一个国家对其他国家显著的影响力。

40. **通货膨胀**：货币价值下降，商品价格上涨，通常由货币供应增长所致。

41. **利率**：借贷的价格，通常体现为未偿贷款的年百分比。

42. **国际收支**：一国与世界其他国家经济交易的指标。一个国家要么是"债权国"，要么是"债务国"。

43. **国际货币基金组织**：一个总部在美国的机构，为维护国际金融稳定和合作而设立；该机构经常向金融不景气的国家借出资金，作为它们改变经济体结构（比如削减开支和将国有企业及资产私有化）的报偿。

44. **国际传播**：金德尔伯格提出的一个观点，认为由于世界经济的相互依存性，金融危机能迅速从一个国家蔓延到其他国家，如同一场"传染病"。

45. **投资者**：希望获取后续金融回报的资本提供者。这里的资本能以股本、债务证券、房地产和商品等形式提供。

46. **日本信贷危机**：20 世纪 80 年代发生在日本的大型金融危机，见证

了股票和房地产市场从繁荣到崩溃的情境。

47. **雷曼兄弟**：一家大型的国际投资银行，于 2008 年 9 月破产，并引发了世界范围的金融危机。

48. **最后贷款人**：一家向濒临破产和崩盘的其他银行或类似金融机构提供贷款的中央银行。

49. **马歇尔计划**：官方名称为"欧洲复兴计划"，是二战之后美国向欧洲提供的一揽子经济援助，价值 130 亿美元。

50. **明斯基模型**：经济学家海曼·明斯基提出的信贷循环模型，后被金德尔伯格进一步拓展。该模型分为五个阶段：移位、繁荣、亢奋、获利回吐和恶性抛售。

51. **货币主义**：经济学领域的一个思想流派，基于"经济体的表现最受货币供应变化的影响"这一观点。

52. **民族主义**：爱国主义的一种极端形式，通常包含"本民族国家的利益高于他国"这一信念。

53. **负反馈环**：当既定规范的干扰造成了放大消极变化的效应时，就有了负反馈环。

54. **诺贝尔奖**：每年都颁发的国际性奖项，用以认可学术界、文化界或科学界的杰出成就。

55. **支付失衡**：一国的出口量超过进口量，就是支付失衡，反之亦然。

56. **比索贬值**：1994 年 12 月，墨西哥政府将比索对美元汇率降低了 15%。其结果出人意料，国际投资者为了撤出资金而大量抛售墨西哥资产，这造成了随即蔓延到亚洲和其他拉美国家的金融危机。

57. **正反馈环**：当既定规范的干扰造成了放大积极变化的效应时，就有了正反馈环。

58. **顺周期性**：该观点认为信贷循环是自我延续的，所以增加信贷供应就可以延长经济繁荣，而缩减信贷供应便会加剧后续的崩盘。

59. **心理学**：对人类心理和行为的研究。

60. **证券**：在上市公司（股票）、借贷关系（债券）或所有权（期权）中标示物主身份的金融协议。

61. **南海泡沫**：历史上最严重的一次金融泡沫之一，与南海公司——成立于 1711 年的英国公司，被准许同南美洲国家进行垄断贸易——股票的剧烈贬值有关。在 1720 年的戏剧性崩盘之前，该公司的股票价格曾飙升到天文数字。

62. **投机者**：向金融资产投资并希望在未来数天或数星期内获得短期回报的人。

63. **（美国）国务院**：美国联邦政府部门，处理美国的国际关系。

64. **股票**：证券的一种，为持有者提供企业的参股份额，赋予其参与企业未来资产分红的权利。

65. **1987 年股市崩盘**：又称"黑色星期一"，发生于 1987 年 10 月 19 日，起因是波斯湾局势紧张，当时道琼斯工业平均指数跌了超过 20%。同一天世界各地的其他股票市场同样损失巨大。

66. **贸易顺差**：一国对世界其他国家的出口量大于进口量，就产生了贸易顺差。

67. **第一次世界大战**：1914 至 1918 年间的世界大战，在同盟国（英国、法国、沙俄和美国）和协约国（德国和奥匈帝国）之间展开。

68. **第二次世界大战**：1939 至 1945 年间的世界大战，主要在"反法西斯同盟"（包括美国、苏联、中国、英国和法国）和轴心国（德国、意大利和日本）之间展开。

人名表

1. **罗伯特·Z.阿利伯**（1930年生），芝加哥大学经济学名誉教授，主要研究领域是对外直接投资的属性。自金德尔伯格过世后，阿利伯编辑并更新了《疯狂、惊恐和崩溃》的最近三个版本。

2. **沃尔特·白芝浩**（1826—1877），英国商人、记者、政治评论家，他就经济学和金融危机的本质撰写了大量作品。

3. **戈登·布朗**（1951年生），前英国首相（2007—2010），前英国财政大臣（1997—2007）。

4. **米歇尔·舍瓦利耶**（1806—1879），法国经济学家、政治家，曾就市场的本质及市场不稳定性发表大量评论。

5. **查尔斯·达尔文**（1809—1882），英国博物学家、科学家，因《物种起源》（1859）一书闻名于世，奠定了现代进化理论的基础。

6. **巴里·艾肯格林**（1952年生），美国经济学家、学者。

7. **尤金·F.法玛**（1939年生），诺贝尔经济学奖得主，主要研究领域是股市行为的分析。他用经验证据表明有效市场假说的可信度，并因此广受赞誉。

8. **米尔顿·弗里德曼**（1912—2006），加利福尼亚大学伯克利分校经济学和政治学教授，他的作品研究了国际货币和金融体系。

9. **约翰·肯尼斯·加尔布雷斯**（1908—2006），著名的经济学家、公共知识分子，在哈佛大学任教超过50年。

10. **蒂莫西·F.盖特纳**（1961年生），前美国财政部长（2009—2013），经济政策的制定者。

11. **罗伯特·吉尔平**（1930 年生），普林斯顿大学政治学与国际事务名誉教授。他的作品聚焦于政治经济的国际维度。

12. **丹尼尔·卡内曼**（1934 年生），普林斯顿大学心理学与公共事务名誉教授。他用实证数据（可由观察证实的数据）的研究挑战了经济学理论中盛行的"理性"决策观点，这也使他成为行为经济学领域的泰斗。

13. **罗伯特·基欧汉**（1941 年生），普林斯顿大学政治学教授，他以金德尔伯格的作品为基础，产出了关于"霸权稳定性"的新观点。

14. **约翰·梅纳德·凯恩斯**（1883—1946），英国经济学家，他的宏观经济理论大大改变了该学科，为如今经济学中的"凯恩斯学派"奠定了基础。

15. **保罗·克鲁格曼**（1953 年生），美国经济学家、诺贝尔奖得主，主要研究领域是国际贸易和经济活动的地理分布。

16. **伯顿·G.马尔基尔**（1932 年生），美国学者、投资者、作家，普林斯顿大学名誉教授，《漫步华尔街》的作者。

17. **阿尔弗雷德·马歇尔**（1842—1924），著名的英国经济学家，被誉为新古典经济学的奠基人之一。

18. **约翰·莫德林**，金融家、经济学家、作家、网络评论员，研究主题是金融市场和经济史。

19. **劳伦斯·G.麦克唐纳**，《常识的溃败：雷曼兄弟破产内幕》（2009）一书的作者，以内部人士的视角剖析了雷曼兄弟银行的破产。他曾任该银行的副总裁。

20. **约翰·斯图尔特·穆勒**（1806—1873），英国经济学家、著名哲学家，对经济学、政治理论和社会理论都做出过广泛贡献。

21. **帕特里克·闵福德**（1943 年生），英国经济学家，卡迪夫大学应用经济学教授。

22. **海曼·明斯基**（1919—1996），圣路易斯华盛顿大学经济学教授，他的作品聚焦于金融危机的本质。

23. **查克·普林斯**（1950 年生），美国商人，跨国金融公司花旗集团的前董事长及首席执行官。

24. **罗伯特·J. 希勒**（1946 年生），诺贝尔经济学奖得主，《非理性繁荣》的作者。他在金融经济学和行为金融学领域的作品质疑了有效市场假说。

25. **罗伯特·斯基德尔斯基**（1939 年生），英国经济史家，华威大学政治经济学名誉教授。

26. **亚当·斯密**（1723—1790），英国经济学家、哲学家，在苏格兰启蒙运动中扮演了关键角色。他的著作《国富论》常被视作经济学学科的奠基之作。

27. **罗伯特·M. 索洛**（1924 年生），诺贝尔经济学奖得主，麻省理工学院经济系名誉教授，因其对经济增长的研究闻名于世。

28. **乔治·索罗斯**（1930 年生），世界最富有、最著名的投资者之一。索罗斯基金管理公司的董事长，对有效市场假说持怀疑态度。

29. **劳伦斯·萨默斯**（1954 年生），美国经济学家，美国财政部长（1999—2001），世界银行首席经济学家（1991—1993）。

30. **纳西姆·尼古拉斯·塔勒布**（1960 年生），黎巴嫩裔美国作家、投资者，他关于随机性和不稳定性本质的作品影响了众多学科领域，包括金融学和哲学。

31. **乔纳森·泰珀**，美国经济学家、作家、"变式知觉"（一个宏观经济学研究组织）的创始人。

32. 阿莫斯·特沃斯基（1937—1996），认知和数学心理学家，他的著作将人类思维处理危机的方式与认知偏差（以印证已有偏见的方式解读信息）联系起来。

33. 维琪·沃德（1969年生），美国记者，《魔鬼赌场：雷曼兄弟内部的友谊、背叛和豪赌》的作者，该书详述了这家投资银行的崩盘。

WAYS IN TO THE TEXT

- Charles Poor Kindleberger was an American economist. He was born in 1910, and died in 2003 at the age of 92.

- His book *Manias, Panics, and Crashes* (1978) analyzes the nature of financial crises,* past and present.

- *Manias, Panics, and Crashes* argues that markets are inherently unstable because of irrational behavior combined with surges in the availability of credit.

Who Was Charles P. Kindleberger?

Charles Poor Kindleberger, author of *Manias, Panics, and Crashes: A History of Financial Crises* (1978), was born in New York City in 1910. During his career as a distinguished economist and academic, he went against conventional wisdom in the 1970s, arguing that the world's financial markets were not as ordered and efficient* as people thought. Kindleberger asserted that markets are unstable, prone to crisis, and at times in need of radical intervention.

Kindleberger's career started with economics* degrees from the University of Pennsylvania and Columbia University, where he earned his doctorate. Before and after World War II* (1939–45) he worked for the US government and helped to draft the Marshall Plan.* This supported the rebuilding of Europe, where infrastructure and industry had been badly damaged in the course of the war. He joined the economics faculty of the Massachusetts Institute of Technology (MIT) in 1948.

In his economic thinking, Kindleberger pursued an international perspective; he was one of the first thinkers to conceive of the economies of individual nations as interdependent. In the 1970s, he noticed certain changes in the international economy that he thought were likely to encourage volatility (that is, instability) and financial crises. The patterns he observed in how economic crises develop laid the foundation for his most influential ideas.

Kindleberger had a vast knowledge of economic history* and wrote using a literary, narrative style totally at odds with the more mathematical analyses of his peers. *Manias, Panics, and Crashes* articulates the inherent instability of the global economy* that was being reawoken in the 1970s. In this sense, his book proved prophetic, predicting many of the twenty-first-century financial meltdowns such as the financial crisis of 2008.*

What Does *Manias, Panics, and Crashes* Say?

Manias, Panics, and Crashes is a classic work of economic history, surveying a vast number of past financial crises. These examples serve Kindleberger's theoretical argument: that each financial crisis is *not* unique. Throughout history, such crises have had much in common. These consistent features and stages of development are what Kindleberger calls a "biologic regularity"* that can be decoded through an examination of economic history.[1] Once this is understood, economic policy can be designed to minimize the damage caused by such chaos.

Kindleberger's argument in *Manias, Panics, and Crashes* rejects the models of economic efficiency that were popular in the 1970s. These theories relied on the idea that investors*—those who provide capital in the hope of profiting from the investment later—act rationally. Instead, Kindleberger saw financial crises as the product of mob psychology among these market players. The wild optimism of a "mania" is typically fed by a surge in the supply of credit, and Kindleberger pinpointed this as a core issue. Easy access to credit enables investors to purchase assets* through debt. During the overoptimistic "mania" of rising prices, such investors get into vast amounts of debt—while assuming that the prices of their assets will continue to rise forever.

When the prices of such assets stop rising (as they inevitably must), a sudden "panic" sets in, leading to a "crash" in asset values. Banks and other financial institutions are liable to go bust as loans are not repaid, and they themselves can be heavily indebted. A wave of insolvency can then develop, and spread to several countries at once through international contagion.* For example, if investors borrow a great deal of money from Mexican banks that they cannot pay back, the banks in Mexico are likely to go bust. American banks might have a lot of money invested in Mexican banks that can no longer be paid back, and suddenly find themselves insolvent as well. British banks might have no investments in Mexico at all, but have huge amounts of money in American banks. So the Mexican crisis could end up bankrupting British banks as a knock-on effect. To make this point, Kindleberger quotes the nineteenth-century economist Alfred Marshall* who said, "The evils of reckless trading are always apt to spread beyond the persons immediately concerned."[2] This is a principal reason for the world's economy being so fragile.

In *Manias, Panics, and Crashes* Kindleberger argues that you cannot stop such crises; you can only contain them. He believed that a single country needed to take charge of the global economy and stabilize it in periods of turbulence. In the aftermath of World War I* (1914–18), when Britain faded as a global power, he thought the United States should take over this role.

Why Does *Manias, Panics, and Crashes* Matter?

Manias, Panics, and Crashes is a famous, incisive analysis of how financial crises work. It first appeared in 1978, when the world was entering a new period of global economic fragility. Over the next 40 years, six of the ten biggest booms and busts in the history of capitalism* (the economic and social system dominant in the West, and increasingly throughout the world, in which business is conducted for private profit) would take place. The sustained popularity of Kindleberger's book shows that international financial crises continue to be a primary issue for the world economy. Since Kindleberger's death in 2003, the economist Robert Z. Aliber* has edited and updated subsequent editions of *Manias, Panics, and Crashes.*

But Kindleberger's text is not just extraordinarily timely. Moving through the long history of financial crises, he creates an entertaining text that still communicates a serious point about the inherent instability of markets. He argues that this volatility will never disappear but can only be managed. The irrational behavior of investors is a constant across time and is still prevalent today.

In 1978, conventional wisdom among economists was based

on the assumption that self-interested market participants like bankers and investors make rational choices. Kindleberger insisted on the constant presence of irrational investing behavior—an unorthodox position in 1978. Since then, entire new fields of economic study have emerged to explore irrational investment decisions—particularly the field of behavioral economics*—and to incorporate psychology* into economic models.These areas have produced Nobel Prize* winners, including Robert J. Shiller,* one of Kindleberger's former students, who described him as having "a great influence on [his] thinking."[3]

Outside academia, Kindleberger's book has also influenced politicians and policymakers, some of whom have had to manage worldwide financial crises. *Manias, Panics, and Crashes* is now essential reading for anyone interested in understanding the market cycle of boom and bust.* The work is also innovative in its style. Kindleberger's literary, narrative voice differs from the mathematics and models often found in economic texts. This makes *Manias, Panics, and Crashes* an engaging read, and a human story.

---

1. Charles P. Kindleberger and Robert Z. Aliber, *Manias, Panics, and Crashes: A History of Financial Crises* (Basingstoke: Palgrave MacMillan, 2015), 20.

2. Kindleberger and Aliber, *Manias, Panics, and Crashes*, 56.

3. Robert J. Shiller, *Irrational Exuberance* (Princeton: Princeton University Press, 2015), 92.

SECTION 1
INFLUENCES

THE AUTHOR AND THE HISTORICAL CONTEXT

KEY POINTS

* *Manias, Panics, and Crashes: A History of Financial Crises* presents a wide-ranging history of financial crises,* and a convincing theory as to why they occur.
* Kindleberger's academic education was enhanced by his work in the US government before and after World War II* (1939–45).
* The 1970s reignited turbulence in the world economy that deeply concerned Kindleberger, giving urgency to the ideas in his book.

Why Read This Text?

Charles P. Kindleberger's *Manias, Panics, and Crashes: A History of Financial Crises* was first published in 1978 and is now in its seventh edition. It has become a classic of economic* history and is still frequently cited in the worlds of academia, finance, politics, and journalism.

The book describes a panoramic history of financial crises going back to the birth of commerce itself. Kindleberger describes in detail the stages such financial crises have had in common. In doing so, he asserts that not all crises are unique—they actually share a "biologic regularity"* that reflects an inherent tendency in the markets to boom and bust,* a cycle that repeats itself in particular stages.[1] In the first phase, an external shock or "displacement"* occurs that leads to economic expansion;

business firms become "euphorically" optimistic and investment surges because credit is easy to obtain.[2] The prices of securities* (financial agreements concerning ownership such as stocks, bonds, and options) and real estate rise dramatically until another shock—perhaps a change in government policy—leads to a pause in the pace of these price increases, which in turn triggers a crash: "There is no plateau, no 'middle ground' ... the rush to sell these securities becomes self-fulfilling and so precipitous that it resembles a panic."[3]

While his dissection of financial crises was not entirely original, Kindleberger was among the first to place such events in an international context. This offered fresh insight that is increasingly relevant to today's global economy. As the US economist Robert M. Solow* says in his introduction to the seventh edition,"Any reader of this book will come away with the distinct notion that larger quantities of liquid capital sloshing around the world should raise the possibility that they will overflow the container."[4] Kindleberger's argument offers potential solutions to slow down or minimize (if not eliminate) such financial crises, and forms a key contribution to this urgent issue in today's political economy.

> *"The three decades since the early 1980s have been the most tumultuous in monetary history in terms of the number, scope, and severity of banking crises."*
>
> —— Charles P. Kindleberger, *Manias, Panics, and Crashes: A History of Financial Crises*

Author's Life

Charles Kindleberger was born in 1910. He graduated from the University of Pennsylvania in 1932 and received a doctorate in economics from Columbia University in 1937, studying under the monetary* theorist James W. Angell. It is notable that Kindleberger's undergraduate education took place during the Great Depression,* a period of unprecedented financial chaos that began in the late 1920s.

After serving in the military during World War II, Kindleberger became chief of the State Department's* Division of German and Austrian Economic Affairs from 1945 to 1947, and advisor to the European Recovery Program from 1947 to 1948. While holding the latter post, he helped design and implement the Marshall Plan,* a massive American effort to revive the European economy after the war. These roles added practical policy experience to Kindleberger's academic learning, and it has been argued that they helped form the ideas described in *Manias, Panics, and Crashes*—particularly his ideas on which countries and international institutions might stabilize the global economy.[5]

In 1948 Kindleberger began an academic career in economics at the Massachusetts Institute of Technology, where he retired as a chaired professor in 1976. He worked as a consultant to the US government many times over this span, and published a great many books and articles. His evolving focus on the international dimensions of financial crises culminated in two texts that are now considered classics: *The World in Depression, 1929–1939* (first published in 1973) and *Manias, Panics, and Crashes* (1978).

Author's Background

Kindleberger trained as an economist during the Great Depression. Within his academic subject, a fierce debate would rage for decades over what exactly had caused this economic catastrophe. Revered economists proposed their own (very different) theories. The British economist John Maynard Keynes,* for example, said the problem had been a chronic lack of consumer demand, which should have been propped up by government spending. The US economist Milton Friedman* argued that it had been the failure of the US Federal Reserve* (the central bank* of the United States) to provide banks with additional funds to meet the demands of depositors. Decades later, Kindleberger would also be drawn to this prominent subject, offering a more international analysis. After World War I* (1914–18), he argued, Great Britain's role as leader of the international economy was fading, just when it was needed most; America, meanwhile, was reluctant to take on the task. The resulting vacuum allowed the world to sink into the Depression.

Kindleberger worked for the US government during its reconstruction of the world economy after World War II. During the 1950s and 1960s, he witnessed (relative) global economic stability— but fundamental changes then took place that greatly concerned him. The international economy of the early 1970s was remarkably volatile, with huge changes in the day-to-day and month-to-month prices of commodities (exchangeable goods), currencies, bonds, stocks* (tradable shares in a business) and real estate, relative to their long-run averages.[6] New technology was clearly playing a role in this: innovations in communications and computing meant that money could travel around the world much more actively, with investors* shifting funds to a foreign center for even a "small anticipated incremental return."[7] These quick movements in capital* only encourage bubbles,* a "bubble" being when the price of an asset* (property) or security* (a financial agreement signifying ownership in a public-traded corporation) increases significantly in a way that cannot be explained by economic fundamentals.[8]

Kindleberger perceived a new global instability reminiscent of the era leading up to the Great Depression, and began to study it in terms of historical precedents. The result was *Manias, Panics, and Crashes*.

---

1. Charles P. Kindleberger and Robert Z. Aliber, *Manias, Panics, and Crashes: A History of Financial Crises* (Basingstoke: Palgrave MacMillan, 2015), 20.
2. Kindleberger and Aliber, *Manias, Panics, and Crashes*, 104.
3. Kindleberger and Aliber, *Manias, Panics, and Crashes*, 20.
4. Kindleberger and Aliber, *Manias, Panics, and Crashes*, VIII.
5. Stephen Meardon, "On Kindleberger and Hegemony: From Berlin to M.I.T. and Back," Bowdoin Digital Commons, September 29, 2013, accessed March 22, 2016, http://digitalcommons.bowdoin. edu/cgi/viewcontent. cgi?article=1003&context=econpapers.
6. Kindleberger and Aliber, *Manias, Panics, and Crashes*, 5.
7. Kindleberger and Aliber, *Manias, Panics, and Crashes*, 25.
8. Kindleberger and Aliber, *Manias, Panics, and Crashes*, 43.

MODULE 2
ACADEMIC CONTEXT

KEY POINTS

* When Kindleberger wrote *Manias, Panics, and Crashes*, economics* departments were largely in thrall to ideas of rational behavior and efficient* outcomes (that is, the idea that an asset's* price is an accurate indication of its value).

* For adherents of the efficient market hypothesis,* international trade promotes efficiency, and any turbulence is part of that process.

* Kindleberger rejected this premise, instead focusing on the irrational elements of international investment that promote instability.

The Work in Its Context

Charles P. Kindleberger wrote the first edition of *Manias, Panics, and Crashes: A History of Financial Crises* in the 1970s. At that time, most economists who studied financial markets were persuaded by the efficient market hypothesis (EMH), which in its purest form rules out the possibility of bubbles*—economically hazardous overpricing—in asset prices (in real estate or securities,* for example).[1]

They had a logical reason for doing so. Led by economists like the Nobel Prize—winner E. F. Fama* and the famous Princeton professor Burton G. Malkiel,* adherents of the EMH asserted that security prices capture all available news and information about their respective companies. If a share price does not do this, these shares have been priced incorrectly, and people will flock to exploit this imbalance (by either buying or selling the incorrectly priced stock),* causing the inefficiency to disappear rapidly. So making significant amounts of money from exploiting these inefficiencies is more or less impossible. The same logic ruled out the possibility of financial bubbles; EMH theory blamed past bubbles on undeveloped, fraud-prone markets, and asserted that such bubbles are unlikely to occur in sophisticated, well-regulated modern markets.[2] Kindleberger argues the opposite in *Manias, Panics, and Crashes*, saying that completely irrational behavior often drives markets and creates crises.

Kindleberger was also one of the few economists of his generation to be skeptical of "monetarists"* like Milton Friedman,* who held sway in the 1950s and 1960s.[3] A monetarist is an economist who believes that the performance of an economy is primarily driven by changes in the supply of money. For monetarists, bubbles can be controlled if the supply of money becomes more restricted—through a rise in interest rates, for example. Kindleberger instead argued that many of the booms in real estate or stock prices occur because of surges in the supply of credit and the inflow of international investment.[4]

> *"The loss of connection with rationality reflects that the investors, lenders, borrowers, and the bank and financial regulators fail to recognize that a crash is always the end game for the mania."*
>
> ——Charles P. Kindleberger, *Manias, Panics, and Crashes: A History of Financial Crises*

Overview of the Field

Kindleberger's study reveals a long history of prominent thinkers who have engaged with the subject of financial crises, and how governments or central banks might be able to contain them. He describes a rich tapestry of contemporary and historic events, all centered upon various surges in prices of securities and real estate, and the subsequent crashes caused by them.[5] Kindleberger frequently quotes "classical economists"* (a group of economists from the eighteenth and nineteenth centuries who theorized about market economies). This group included figures like the economist and philosopher John Stuart Mill* and the economist Walter Bagehot,* both British, who expounded concepts of market instability that Kindleberger would develop.[6]

For example, it was Mill who first raised the question as to how much credit households, firms, and governments can command at a given time.[7] This question is central to Kindleberger's investigation. He also consistently cites the "Bagehot doctrine,"* arguing that central banks must provide an unlimited amount of credit to solvent banks during a crisis, at a penalty interest rate (this "penalty" ensuring that the central bank will truly be used as the "lender of last resort.")*[8] Kindleberger pushes this idea further, arguing that such help must also include insolvent banks (banks that cannot return cash invested by their customers).[9]

Kindleberger was writing at a time when the efficient market hypothesis was at the height of its popularity. In his eyes, at the heart of this theory is the assumption of "rational expectations":

that investors react to changes in economic variables as if they are always fully aware of the long-term implications of each of these changes.[10] For Kindleberger, this idea is utterly discredited by history:"Rationality is an a priori assumption about the way the world should work rather than a description of the way the world has actually worked."[11]

Academic Influences

While the efficient market hypothesis was widely popular in the 1970s, the economist Hyman Minsky's* "financial instability hypothesis"* (developed in the 1960s) was remarkably out of fashion. This is understandable, as he essentially argued the opposite case: that the financial system in a market economy is inherently unstable, fragile, and prone to crisis.[12] Minsky supported this view with a theory of credit cycles that is perhaps the primary influence on Kindleberger's book. Essentially, Minsky believed that supplies of credit are pro-cyclical:* that is, increases in the supply of credit prolong the expansion of the boom, and decreases in the supply of credit intensify the subsequent crash.[13] The "Minsky model"* is an extremely useful tool for explaining financial crises,* past and present, as so many of them follow a surge in real estate prices that stems from an increase in the supply of credit.[14]

Minsky's model follows in the tradition of the same classical economists who so interested Kindleberger,[15] in particular, the "classical" ideas of market instability; these earlier economists used terms like "overtrading" to describe a mania, and said that it leads to a "revulsion" period (panic) and ultimately "discredit" (a crash). They also concentrated on the variability in the supply of credit, a focus amplified by Minsky. Kindleberger can be seen as a more recent member of this intellectual school of thought, adapting an existing tradition to a more international context.

1. *Economist*, "Of Manias, Panics, and Crashes," July 19, 2003, accessed March 22, 2016, http://www.economist.com/node/1923462.

2. *Economist*, "Of Manias, Panics, and Crashes."

3. Charles P. Kindleberger and Robert Z. Aliber, *Manias, Panics, and Crashes: A History of Financial Crises* (Basingstoke: Palgrave MacMillan, 2015), 2.

4. Kindleberger and Aliber, *Manias, Panics, and Crashes*, 25.

5. Kindleberger and Aliber, *Manias, Panics, and Crashes*, 25.

6. Kindleberger and Aliber, *Manias, Panics, and Crashes*, 27.

7. Kindleberger and Aliber, *Manias, Panics, and Crashes*, 85.

8. Kindleberger and Aliber, *Manias, Panics, and Crashes*, 278.

9. Kindleberger and Aliber, *Manias, Panics, and Crashes*, 323.

10. Kindleberger and Aliber, *Manias, Panics, and Crashes*, 53.

11. Kindleberger and Aliber, *Manias, Panics, and Crashes*, 55.

12. Kindleberger and Aliber, *Manias, Panics, and Crashes*, 27.

13. Kindleberger and Aliber, *Manias, Panics, and Crashes*, 2.

14. Kindleberger and Aliber, *Manias, Panics, and Crashes*, 27.

15. Kindleberger and Aliber, *Manias, Panics, and Crashes*, 39.

MODULE 3
THE PROBLEM

KEY POINTS

- The main question engaging Kindleberger's academic peers in the mid-1970s was how markets promote efficient* outcomes.

- Many economists debated the reasons for the catastrophic economic downturn of the late 1920s and 1930s, the Great Depression,* and followed the "demand-driven" theory of the English economist John Maynard Keynes* (according to which a faltering economy can be stimulated by government spending), or the money-supply theory of the US economist Milton Friedman* (according to which an economy can be stabilized through controls of the amount of money in circulation).

- Kindleberger took a more international perspective on the Great Depression, and thought that recent developments in the world economy foster even greater instability.

Core Question

The core questions that Charles P. Kindleberger seeks to answer in *Manias, Panics, and Crashes: A History of Financial Crises* are: Why do financial crises* happen? Why do they now seem to be growing bigger and more common? And what can be done about them? "If many financial crises have a stylized form," he asks, "should there be a standard policy response?"[1]

Kindleberger saw that most bubbles*—past and present—are fed by a surge in the supply of credit, but there was also a new source of global fragility that was unique to his age. Global "payment imbalances"* developed in the late 1960s, and continued through the next several decades.[2] To explain what a payment imbalance is, we might consider the case of Saudi Arabia.

In the 1970s, many of the world's top oil-producing nations agreed to purposefully decrease the production of crude oil—a move that drove up international oil prices, greatly enhancing the profit margins for oil producers. The oil-producing nation Saudi Arabia was exporting far more to other countries than it was importing, which created a large "payment imbalance" between it and the nations importing its oil. The huge surplus* wealth that Saudi Arabia gained from trading with these countries could then be invested globally to earn further returns, in whatever assets* the Saudis preferred—they could invest in Thai securities* (tradable assets such as stocks)* one day, helping to drive up the price in that market, before suddenly selling them and reinvesting the proceeds in Brazilian securities—or any other worldwide investment that appealed at that moment.

So, this wandering money travels around the world in search of higher profits as a "cross-border investment flow"* (financial arrangements that cross national borders, typically taking the form of loans, acquisitions, or credit). There are big currency issues in cross-border investment flows.[3] If money from around the world rushes into the Brazilian stock market, the value of the Brazilian currency itself will also rise. If Brazilian securities peak and no longer earn large returns, all those global investors* may sell at once—so the price of Brazilian securities *and* the price of the currency will crash as investors suddenly run for the exits, trying to sell their assets before their inevitable and rapid depreciation (loss in value).Thus, such investment flows can leave a country with both a financial *and* a currency crisis.*4

> "Nevertheless despite the lack of perfect comparability across periods, the conclusion is unmistakable that banking crises have been more extensive and pervasive."
>
> ——Charles P. Kindleberger, *Manias, Panics, and Crashes: A History of Financial Crises*

The Participants

For adherents of the efficient market hypothesis* (the idea that asset prices, including stock prices, capture all available information about that asset)—so popular in economics* departments during the 1970s—these cross-border investment flows reflect global efficiency in the long term. Global money, they would argue, is following good, and perhaps underpriced, investments worldwide, and so raising their price to an efficient equilibrium while lowering the price of less worthy investments ("equilibrium" here refers to the idea that the prices of assets settle to reflect their true, balanced, value). It may be a bumpy ride, but stability can be achieved just by letting international markets function, unhampered by financial regulation.*

Monetarists* like Milton Friedman* (those who believe that a market's performance is closely associated with the amount of money in circulation in an economy) admit that markets can get dangerously overheated, and see interest rates*—the price of borrowing—as a means of creating stability. If a government can control the domestic supply of money by raising interest rates, for example, it can restrain overinflated markets: the higher interest raises the price of borrowing money, so fewer people will do so. Ultimately this lowers demand across an economy. As Kindleberger puts it, "Many monetarists insist that many, perhaps most, of the cyclical difficulties of the past have resulted from mismanagement of the monetary mechanism."[5]

A string of financial crises over the past few decades has turned up the volume of this debate, with many more voices joining in. The economist Robert Z.Aliber*—who took over the role of editing and updating *Manias, Panics, and Crashes* after Kindleberger's death—notes in the seventh edition, the 2008 global financial crisis* and the ensuing recession has inspired a spate of books on the topic. They tend to be written by three types of authors: journalists, academics, and "insiders" who have worked in finance.[6] Overall, Aliber is less than impressed: "The shortcoming of most of these books is that they give no explanation for why the crisis occurred when it did, nor do they have an explanation for why some countries were involved but not others."[7]

The Contemporary Debate

In stark contrast to the popular theories of his contemporaries, Kindleberger came to a very different view of the nature of financial crises. Drawing on the economist Hyman Minksy's* relatively unpopular financial instability hypothesis,* according to which economic prosperity leads to reckless investment behavior, Kindleberger developed Minsky's argument that the reckless use of a credit cycle leads to a mania, panic, and an inevitable crash.

A wave of global financial crises commenced soon after the first publication of *Manias, Panics, and Crashes*, at a time when the authority of the efficient market hypothesis was already starting to dwindle. For example, Daniel Kahneman* and Amos Tversky*— researchers in the field of the human mind and economic behavior—published a study on "behavioral decision theory" in 1979, claiming that investors are systematically overconfident in their capacity to predict future stock prices and corporate earnings.[8] Their conclusion anticipates the emergence of behavioral finance,* a field that turns to the discipline of psychology* to answer questions about economic behavior, and which has come to seriously challenge the efficiency market hypothesis, while also supporting Kindleberger's claims of irrational, "herd" behavior among investors.

That said, when *Manias, Panics, and Crashes* was first published in 1978, Friedman's monetarism was still convincing major policymakers. From 1979–82, the Federal Reserve* (the central bank of the United States) began to limit the growth of the money supply in the US economy in an effort to tame high inflation* (a fall in the value of money, and rise in the value of prices); this effort became known as the great "monetarist experiment," and had decidedly mixed results.[9] Nonetheless, monetary tools (basically, measures to control the supply of money in an economy) remained quite popular, and are still seen as a powerful way to tame the larger fluctuations of a boom-and-bust* business cycle.

Finally, in 1978 there were economists and prominent opinion-makers who claimed that increased regulation was the way to prevent financial crises—indeed, there are *always* people making this claim.[10] Kindleberger actually disagrees with this policy, asserting something that is almost heresy: that seeing financial institutions such as banks as responsible for a financial crisis is to mistake "the symptoms of the crisis for the causes."[11] In Kindleberger's view, even if these firms *were* responsible for the crash, banking "is difficult to regulate because new institutions develop that circumvent the regulations."[12]

---

1. Charles P. Kindleberger and Robert Z. Aliber, *Manias, Panics, and Crashes: A History of Financial Crises*, (Basingstoke: Palgrave MacMillan, 2015), 235.

2. Kindleberger and Aliber, *Manias, Panics, and Crashes*, 219.

3. Kindleberger and Aliber, *Manias, Panics, and Crashes*, 220.

4. Kindleberger and Aliber, *Manias, Panics, and Crashes*, 222.

5. Kindleberger and Aliber, *Manias, Panics, and Crashes*, 28.

6. Kindleberger and Aliber, *Manias, Panics, and Crashes*, 16–17.

7. Kindleberger and Aliber, *Manias, Panics, and Crashes*, 17.

8. Burton G. Malkiel, "The Efficient Market Hypothesis and Its Critics," *Journal of Economic Perspectives* 17, no. 1 (Winter, 2003): 63.

9. David R. Hakes and David C. Rose, "The 1979–1982 Monetary Policy Experiment: Monetarist, Anti-Monetarist, or Quasi-Monetarist?", *Journal of Post Keynesian Economics* 15, no. 2 (Winter, 1992–3): 281–8.

10. Kindleberger and Aliber, *Manias, Panics, and Crashes*, 239.

11. Kindleberger and Aliber, *Manias, Panics, and Crashes*, 3.

12. Kindleberger and Aliber, *Manias, Panics, and Crashes*, 28.

THE AUTHOR'S CONTRIBUTION

KEY POINTS

- Kindleberger asserts that irrational investment behavior combined with a surge in the supply of credit creates financial crises,* which then spread internationally.

- Kindleberger's argument leans heavily on the economist Hyman Minsky's* "financial instability hypothesis,"* which sees financial crises arising from the increased availability of credit in times of economic prosperity.

- *Manias, Panics, and Crashes* broke new ground as the first book of its kind to examine financial meltdowns from an international perspective.

Author's Aims

The primary objective of Charles P. Kindleberger's *Manias, Panics, and Crashes: A History of Financial Crises* is to put the economic assumption of "rationality" on trial: "The central issue is whether the markets in securities* and real estate are always rational, or whether speculation can be destabilizing."[1] For Kindleberger, the idea that investors* always act "rationally" is clearly a myth, debunked by the pure weight of historical evidence. Those who believe otherwise, such as adherents of the efficient market hypothesis,* according to which the price of assets* on the financial markets eventually reflects their true value if the market is left to its own devices, are living in a fantasyland.[2]

Kindleberger aims to prove that the source of "manias"

(a buying spree of financial products that drives up prices) is a surge in the supply of credit and cross-border investment flows* (a financial arrangement such as a loan or acquisition) during times of economic boom.[3] Inevitably, the tide turns and the price of securities and real estate (driven by the easy availability of money through credit) begins to decline, provoking a "panic" and then a "crash."[4] Finally, Kindleberger shows that there are no easy solutions to this predicament, which has grown to global proportions.[5] He ultimately makes a case for a "lender of last resort"* on an international level—that is to say, a financial institution (or entire country) that can bail out banks around the world and so prevent the collapse of the global financial system.[6]

Part of Kindleberger's purpose is to unlock the relationship between the irrational behavior of investors and the institutions they use, as such behavior seems to depend so much on this.[7] For example, he notes that in times of economic "euphoria" it is not only investors who become overly optimistic, pointing out that "authorities recognize that something exceptional is happening and while they are mindful of earlier manias, 'this time it's different,' and they have extensive explanations for why it is different."[8] It was not very long ago, after all, that Gordon Brown,* then the United Kingdom's chancellor of the exchequer (chief of the ministry of finance) declared "an end to [the] boom and bust"* cycle.[9] The 2008 global financial crisis* proved how wrong this grand pronouncement was.

> *"A general collapse of credit, however short the time it lasts, is more fearful than the most terrible earthquake."*
>
> —— Michel Chevalier, *Lettres sur l'Amérique du Nord*

Approach

Kindleberger's approach has been compared to that of the influential English evolutionary theorist Charles Darwin,* in that he moves through the history of financial turmoil "collecting, examining, and classifying interesting specimens."[10] There is the sense that Kindleberger isn't just cherry-picking "specimens" that support a preconceived position, but instead forms an argument based on historical evidence.[11] He ends up with a unique—and uniquely insightful—narrative that reveals underlying and unifying causes of financial crises.

A major cornerstone of Kindleberger's approach is to emphasize, as the economist Hyman Minsky did before him, that changes in the supply of credit are "pro-cyclical."*[12] This means that during periods of economic boom, credit becomes much more plentiful and easy to obtain as investors experience "euphoria" about future financial prospects.[13] The supply of credit is then sharply reduced when the euphoria begins to dissipate, and recession begins to set in (as in the American "credit crunch"* of 2007, when credit became difficult to obtain). This decrease in credit greatly intensifies the crash when it finally comes, often threatening the entire financial system with bankruptcy.[14] It is this perspective that leads Kindleberger to argue for an international "lender of last resort," which can provide the bailouts necessary to prevent total financial collapse.

Contribution in Context

It is common for people to criticize Kindleberger's argument as not wholly original.[15] The "Minsky model,"* which carefully argued that an economy's supply of credit is the primary source of booms and busts, existed well before Kindleberger's book. Kindleberger's originality was to extend this perspective to an international context, noting, for example, "that the failure of a bank in Ohio led to shortages of credit in Hamburg and Scandinavia."[16] Kindleberger wanted to reveal the international contagion* of financial crises, as "historically euphoria has often spread from one country to others," and, likewise, the resulting panics and crashes.[17] Another example of Kindleberger's global perspective was his keen awareness of international currency speculators,* who often sell off a country's currency as its boom turns to bust; this can augment a country's financial crisis with a currency crisis*—when a currency falls in value, discouraging potential investors (among other consequences).

In expanding on Minsky's ideas, Kindleberger also examined the stages of a financial crisis in much greater detail. First there is the "displacement,"* in which the removal of regulations of banking practices or investments leads to a boom, or a new technology or innovation radically improves profitability in a market (the boom in information technologies in the late 1990s following the invention of the Internet, for example, saw a surge of investment in Internet companies).[18] This typically leads to an increase in the price of such assets, creating a "euphoria" that draws more investors in.[19] A "mania" develops with super-high prices fuelled by speculation (investors seeking profits), until there is a significant event that signals the end of the boom: the failure of a bank or major firm, for example.[20] The "revulsion" phase then begins: there is a mass, panicked sell-off, and prices plummet.[21] This is a framework drawn from history, but Kindleberger explores it with an accuracy that was remarkably fresh when it first appeared. It has proved to resonate since with academics, financiers, and policymakers.

1. Charles P. Kindleberger and Robert Z. Aliber, *Manias, Panics, and Crashes: A History of Financial Crises*, (Basingstoke: Palgrave MacMillan, 2015), 27.

2. Kindleberger and Aliber, *Manias, Panics, and Crashes*, 55.

3. Kindleberger and Aliber, *Manias, Panics, and Crashes*, 31, 78, 201.

4. Kindleberger and Aliber, *Manias, Panics, and Crashes*, 20.

5. Kindleberger and Aliber, *Manias, Panics, and Crashes*, 23.

6. Kindleberger and Aliber, *Manias, Panics, and Crashes*, 279.

7. Kindleberger and Aliber, *Manias, Panics, and Crashes*, vii.

8. Kindleberger and Aliber, *Manias, Panics, and Crashes*, 41.

9. James Kirkup, "Gordon Brown admits he was wrong to claim he had ended 'boom and bust,'" *Telegraph*, November 21, 2008, accessed March 22, 2016, http://www.telegraph.co.uk/finance/recession/3497533/Gordon-Brown-admits-he-was-wrong-to-claim-he-had-ended-boom-and-bust.html.

10. Kindleberger and Aliber, *Manias, Panics, and Crashes*, vii.

11. Kindleberger and Aliber, *Manias, Panics, and Crashes*, vii.

12. Kindleberger and Aliber, *Manias, Panics, and Crashes*, 1.

13. Kindleberger and Aliber, *Manias, Panics, and Crashes*, 84, 104.

14. Kindleberger and Aliber, *Manias, Panics, and Crashes*, 1, 245.

15. *Economist*, "Of Manias, Panics, and Crashes," July 19, 2003, accessed March 22, 2016, http://www.economist.com/node/1923462.

16. Kindleberger and Aliber, *Manias, Panics, and Crashes*, 2.

17. Kindleberger and Aliber, *Manias, Panics, and Crashes*, 44.

18. Kindleberger and Aliber, *Manias, Panics, and Crashes*, 72.

19. Kindleberger and Aliber, *Manias, Panics, and Crashes*, 41.

20. Kindleberger and Aliber, *Manias, Panics, and Crashes*, 46.

21. Kindleberger and Aliber, *Manias, Panics, and Crashes*, 46.

SECTION 2
IDEAS

MAIN IDEAS

KEY POINTS

- Kindleberger focuses his study on irrational behavior by investors,* surges in credit, cross-border investment flows,* and how investment manias quickly turn into panics and then crashes.

- Through a wealth of historical examples, Kindleberger theorizes that there is a "biologic regularity"* to financial crises,* showing that they share the same stages of development; he then suggests what measures can be taken to contain them.

- Kindleberger thought that the field of economics* had become too mathematical; he used a "literary economics" with a strong narrative to communicate his argument in human terms.

Key Themes

Charles P. Kindleberger's *Manias, Panics, and Crashes: A History of Financial Crises* identifies the common elements that lead to major economic breakdowns: irrational behavior by investors, surges in credit, cross-border investment flows, and investment manias that quickly turn into panics and then crashes. Kindleberger finds that booms in the prices of both stocks* and real estate are often accompanied by surges in the supply of credit and cross-border investment flows.[1] He also examines the relation between monetary authorities (the central bank in each country) and private-sector banks, and lenders. He concludes that the problem is not that large banks are unregulated, but that money can be too easy to borrow.[2] Such an expansive monetary environment is what causes banks to create more credit themselves and to purchase more loans—and eventually to go bust when the optimistic mania turns into a panic and crash.[3]

Kindleberger also dissects the stages of boom and bust.* This is the optimistic euphoria within a country's real estate or stock market that leads to speculators* borrowing more and more money to finance more investments, hoping for substantial short-term gains. As long as credit is easy to obtain, such professional speculators are always able to borrow more money to pay interest on outstanding loans. One ominous question echoes through Kindleberger's argument time and time again: "Where will borrowers get the money to pay the interest on their outstanding indebtedness if there are not enough new loans to provide the money?"[4] This leads him to his final theme: the importance of a "lender of last resort,"* which in today's global economy is needed at an international level to bail out large banks and firms to prevent or reduce the knock-on effects of their failure on the wider economy.

> *"There is a biologic regularity in the pattern in each of these manias even though there are differences in details."*
>
> —— Charles P. Kindleberger, *Manias, Panics, and Crashes: A History of Financial Crises*

Exploring the Ideas

For Kindleberger, manias simply cannot be stopped. Once the financial world's "insiders" (investors with privileged access to the latest trends) start making money within a particular market, it's not long before "a follow-the-leader process develops as firms and households see that the investors make a lot of money." The reason behind this is emotive, not rational; there is "nothing as disturbing to one's well-being and judgment as to see a friend get rich. Unless it is a non-friend get richer."[5] These outsiders (Kindleberger's "non-friends") pour their money in, momentum develops, and soon a bubble* forms.[6] If credit is easily available, people will borrow wildly in order to make the most of the boom—and believe that this time, the good times will last (because "this time it's different").[7] This recklessness pushes the bubble further, but because the behavior of every participant within it *seems* rational, no one can tell that the situation has become manic.[8] Cross-border investment flows (through international financial transactions like loans) add to the demand for "hot" investments, driving prices up even further. Nonetheless, authorities such as countries' central banks are often loathe to intervene, and take the "punch bowl away from the party just as the party is getting going," because they fear the public will react unfavorably to government interference.[9]

"The central question," Kindleberger writes, "is whether a central bank can restrain the instability in the supply of credit and slow speculation down to avoid its dangerous extension."[10] He doubts that central banks are "omniscient and omnipotent" (that is, all-knowing and all-powerful) enough to do this. That said, an international "lender of last resort" could help reduce the impact of such crises. When a banking crisis hits and banks are unexpectedly short of cash, they must sell their securities* to raise the necessary funds.[11] If all the banks are selling their securities at once, while all the other investors are likewise "running for the exits," then their capital* will not be significantly increased by these sales as prices will have already crashed. These banks might suddenly find themselves insolvent (that is, unable to meet their financial obligations, such as to honor debts).[12]

What a "lender of last resort" can do is extend cash loans to distressed institutions to see them through their cash crises, asking them to pay the loans back when the prices of their securities recover. This spares the overall economy much of the turbulence and chaos of a more severe crash.

Language and Expression

Kindleberger saw himself as a "literary economist" who relied upon historical texts and narrative, much in the mold of the famous eighteenth-century philosopher and economist Adam Smith.*[13]

Although fairly technical wording does often appear in Kindleberger's writing, the technical material of *Manias, Panics, and Crashes* is mixed with a precise and enjoyable prose. It is also pitched at a readable tone of entertaining historical anecdote. For example, Kindleberger points out that some investors cannot resist investing in a known asset* bubble: prices are going up and they are convinced they will sell before the crash comes. To illustrate this point, he cites a banker who invested £500 (around £100,000 or $140,000 in today's terms) in the famous South Sea bubble* of 1720, saying, "When the rest of the world are mad, we must imitate them in some measure."[14] (During the South Sea bubble, shares in the British South Sea Company, granted a monopoly on trade with South America, rose to astronomical heights before crashing dramatically, damaging the British economy.) He follows this immediately with a quote from Chuck Prince,* then the chair of the US multinational finance corporation Citigroup, who said before the stock market crash of 2008* that "You have to keep dancing as long as the music is playing."[15]

This playfully suggests that such behavior in the world of finance has been consistent over time; and the pairing of these quotes gives them much greater impact than either would have had on its own. Together they speak directly to Kindleberger's primary point—that a "biologic regularity" exists within the manias, panics, and crashes of economic history.

---

1. Charles P. Kindleberger and Robert Z. Aliber, *Manias, Panics, and Crashes: A History of Financial Crises* (Basingstoke: Palgrave MacMillan, 2015), 3.

2. Kindleberger and Aliber, *Manias, Panics, and Crashes*, 3.

3. Kindleberger and Aliber, *Manias, Panics, and Crashes*, 20.

4. Kindleberger and Aliber, *Manias, Panics, and Crashes*, 52.

5. Kindleberger and Aliber, *Manias, Panics, and Crashes*, 43.

6. Kindleberger and Aliber, *Manias, Panics, and Crashes*, 43.

7. Kindleberger and Aliber, *Manias, Panics, and Crashes*, 41.

8. Kindleberger and Aliber, *Manias, Panics, and Crashes*, 63.

9. Kindleberger and Aliber, *Manias, Panics, and Crashes*, 111.

10. Kindleberger and Aliber, *Manias, Panics, and Crashes*, 101.

11. Kindleberger and Aliber, *Manias, Panics, and Crashes*, 281.

12. Kindleberger and Aliber, *Manias, Panics, and Crashes*, 281.

13. Michael H. Turk, *The Idea of History in Constructing Economics* (Abingdon: Routledge, 2016), 191.

14. Kindleberger and Aliber, *Manias, Panics, and Crashes*, 57.

15. Kindleberger and Aliber, *Manias, Panics, and Crashes*, 57.

MODULE 6
SECONDARY IDEAS

KEY POINTS

• Kindleberger was concerned about how financial crises* often create currency crises* as well; he also saw that "positive feedback loops"*—self-amplifying cycles—within economies can make crises difficult to prevent.

• These secondary ideas build on Kindleberger's main points, illuminating the complex nature of financial crises.

• Currency crises underscore the international dimension to financial crises, while "positive feedback loops" reveal their durability.

Other Ideas

The secondary themes of Charles P. Kindleberger's *Manias, Panics, and Crashes: A History of Financial Crises* are the relationship between financial crises and currency crises, and what are known as "positive feedback loops." Besides the growth of cross-border investment flows,* Kindleberger saw other reasons for rising instability in the global economy. One was the United States's abandonment of the "gold standard"* in 1971.[1] The "gold standard" is a monetary system whereby a nation's currency has a value directly linked to a specific amount of gold. In 1934 the American government declared an ounce of gold to be worth $35, and held this ratio in place until 1971.

When a government's currency notes are backed by the inherent value of a precious metal like this, there are many stabilizing advantages. One is that the value of the currency will not rise or fall so turbulently in relation to other currencies (as it is anchored to gold, and so is "fixed").* When the American dollar left the "gold standard" in 1971, it entered a "free-floating"* arrangement in which its value became much more strongly determined by international currency markets and their volatile forces of supply and demand.

Secondly, of all the "manias" from history examined by Kindleberger, the 1980s asset* bubble* in Japan* is among the most frequently mentioned. This example provides telling insights about the "positive feedback loops" of the boom-and-bust* cycle that make it so difficult to prevent: a boom creates more booms—in a way that seems failsafe and practically irresistible, thereby boosting investors'* and speculators'* confidence—while a bust creates self-feeding negativity that makes the crash worse and worse.[2]

> "By 1989 the chatter in Tokyo was that the market value of the land under the Imperial Palace was greater than the market value of all the real estate in California."
>
> —— Charles P. Kindleberger, *Manias, Panics, and Crashes: A History of Financial Crises*

Exploring the Ideas

Because of America's prominence in global capitalism* over the last decades, the dollar's gold standard was an anchor of stability for the entire global system ("capitalism" here refers to the social and economic system, increasingly dominant throughout the world, in which business and investment is conducted for private profit). Other countries could "peg" their currencies to the US dollar, continually revaluing their own respective currencies to maintain stable ratios of exchange with America (the dollar itself conferring a stable value in terms of gold). This provided much calmer currency exchange worldwide. The elaborate "Bretton Woods system,"* for example, in operation between 1945 and 1971, coordinated monetary management between the US, Canada, Western Europe, Australia, and Japan. It used the bedrock of the American gold standard to create stable exchange rates between these countries.

This dynamic was radically destabilized in 1971, however, when the US departure from the gold standard ended the Bretton Woods system. The dollar entered a "floating currency arrangement," whereby the international currency markets determined how valuable it was in relation to other currencies. International currency speculators can wreak havoc in such a market: if the mood of the crowd, seeking short-term profits, determines that the dollar is becoming less valuable in relation, say, to the British pound, a momentum can develop and soon the dollar can be devalued on the international marketplace for no reason other than that the irrational "herd" of speculators do not want to be left with a currency no one else wants.[3] Kindleberger predicted that America's change to a "floating" currency arrangement—disconnected from the stabilizing effects of the gold standard—would create a new source of financial instability.[4]

In the second half of the 1980s, the growth in the supplies of money and credit in Japan were extreme, and included an influx of global investment, which led to a boom in stock* and real estate prices.[5] Japanese banks owned large amounts of these two assets, so as the prices of stocks and real estate increased, the capital* of these banks also increased.The banks used this increase in capital to lend money to borrowers investing in stocks or real estate. Supplying money in the form of credit drove up the price of these assets even further, which in turn provided the lending banks with yet more capital (as the value of their own holdings increased again).[6] Through this process, "Japan had developed the financial equivalent of a 'perpetual motion machine.'" The more the banks lent out, the more they saw the price of their own assets rise, which gave them more money to lend out again.[7]

Naturally, when the crash finally hit, this "perpetual motion machine" began to work in reverse; stock and real estate prices fell, which meant the banks had less capital to loan money, which led to further reductions in price.[8] Japan's recession was severe and prolonged; it has not seen anything resembling such high growth and prosperity since.

Overlooked

While Kindleberger makes a compelling case for the dangers of free-floating currencies, it is possible to argue that this arrangement actually has benefits in terms of calming a "mania."

Economists like Milton Friedman* theorized that controlling a nation's money supply (the amount of money in circulation) is the best tool for controlling its economic performance. In boom times, a country can raise its interest rates.* This makes the cost of borrowing higher and therefore shrinks the money supply, restraining an overheated (and perhaps manic) economy. During recessionary times, a country might lower its interest rates, allowing money to be borrowed more cheaply and so providing a direct stimulus to the economy (when people spend the money they have borrowed).

But if a country is trying to maintain a fixed exchange rate with other countries (for example, by "pegging" their currency to the dollar), it is unable to increase or decrease the money supply in this way, as such a move will affect international supply and demand for that currency. If Argentina lowers its interest rates, say, and so increases its money supply, this will also increase the international supply of Argentinian pesos, making the currency less scarce. Everything else being equal, the value of the Argentinian peso will fall under these circumstances—a result acceptable under a free-floating system but not under a fixed one. In a fixed system, a particular pegged value of the Argentinian peso must be maintained by international agreement, which can prevent the government from lowering interest rates when it (perhaps desperately) needs to (if such a move will displace its currency from its agreed, pegged, international worth).

Therefore, a free-floating system can provide a country with the freedom to control its own money supply through interest rates—it is not obligated to maintain the value of its currency at any preordained, pegged level. Directly reducing the supply of money during excessively rapid growth can help weaken a boom, and so a free-floating exchange rate can actually encourage financial stability.

---

1. Charles P. Kindleberger and Robert Z. Aliber, *Manias, Panics, and Crashes: A History of Financial Crises*, (Basingstoke: Palgrave MacMillan, 2015), 1.

2. Kindleberger and Aliber, *Manias, Panics, and Crashes*, 206.

3. Kindleberger and Aliber, *Manias, Panics, and Crashes*, 55–6.

4. Kindleberger and Aliber, *Manias, Panics, and Crashes*, 1.

5. Kindleberger and Aliber, *Manias, Panics, and Crashes*, 207.

6. Kindleberger and Aliber, *Manias, Panics, and Crashes*, 206.

7. Kindleberger and Aliber, *Manias, Panics, and Crashes*, 207.

8. Kindleberger and Aliber, *Manias, Panics, and Crashes*, 208.

MODULE 7
ACHIEVEMENT

KEY POINTS

* *Manias, Panics, and Crashes* is widely regarded as a pioneering study of financial crises,* and has become a classic in the field of economics.*

* Prophetically, *Manias, Panics, and Crashes* was published just before a series of intense financial crises, and offered observers a persuasive explanation as to what caused them.

* It could be argued that Kindleberger's thesis, which refutes the economic approach known as monetarism,* may not consider thoroughly enough how controlling the supply of money can be a stabilizing force in the world economy.

Assessing the Argument

The first edition of Charles P. Kindleberger's *Manias, Panics, and Crashes: A History of Financial Crises* was published in 1978. It is fair to say that—even though the book leans on the work of his predecessor, the economist Hyman Minsky*—Kindleberger achieved his ambitions and created his own classic book on financial catastrophes on an international scale. His immense weight of learning is evident throughout, not only through well-chosen examples of financial crises and contemporary quotes, but also in the way he presents them within a description of the stages of boom and bust.*

As global economies grow increasingly interdependent, there remains much to be learned from Kindleberger's ideas of "international propagation" (or contagion),* according to which "financial crises often ricochet from one country to another."[1] This groundbreaking perspective has been increasingly validated and cited since 1978; a recent and wide-ranging assessment of Kindleberger's achievement, funded by the European Union, was another notable moment in this process of critical affirmation.[2] Kindleberger also succeeded in expressing his ideas with engaging writing, earning him the moniker "literary economist." The economics editor of Princeton University Press referred to his book as a "model for economists who want to reach a wider audience," thanks to his refined yet accessible style.[3]

Since 1978, *Manias, Panics, and Crashes* has gone through seven editions to date, each building on the last—the most recent editions have been edited and updated by Robert Z.Aliber—and Kindleberger has been repeatedly praised as a giant in his field. The text is still frequently quoted by investors, academics, politicians, and journalists. The British newspaper the *Financial Times*, for example, referred to Kindleberger as "the pre-eminent historian of financial crises" almost 10 years after his death in 2003.[4] The popular financial book *Code Red: How to Protect Your Savings From the Coming Crisis* (2013) by economists John Maudlin* and Jonathan Tepper* calls Kindleberger's classic text "the bible on bubbles."*[5]

"More manias, panics, and crashes may plague us, but readers of this book will at least have been inoculated."

——Robert M. Solow, foreword to *Manias, Panics, and Crashes: A History of Financial Crises*

Achievement in Context

Undoubtedly, part of the great success of *Manias, Panics, and Crashes* is down to timing.When the first edition was published in 1978, some of the biggest bubbles and crashes in economic history were about to take place. Throughout the 1970s there had been a surge in loans (that is, credit) from international banks to governments and government-owned firms in Mexico, Brazil, Argentina, and 10 other developing countries[6] ("developing" here refers to their state of national prosperity, considered less advanced than in "developed" nations such as the United States or Germany). The external indebtedness of these countries was increasing by 20 percent a year, and consequently, in 1982, they defaulted on their combined debts of $800 billion.[7] This sparked financial crises within each of these nations, as well as in the international banks that had funded them. As the Lebanese American author and investor Nassim Nicholas Taleb* puts it so memorably in his book *Black Swan* (2007): "In the summer of 1982, large American banks lost close to all their past earnings (cumulatively), about everything they ever made in the history of American banking—everything," due to this unexpected wave of defaults.*[8]

Global crises followed in other parts of the world, including the bubble in stocks and real estate in Japan (1985–9);* the East Asian crisis* (1997); the dot.com boom* in the American stock market concerning technology companies (1995–9); and the bubble in real estate in the US, UK, Spain, Ireland, and Iceland (2002–7). Each crisis was triggered by a huge surge in credit, and, as the 2015 edition of *Manias, Panics, and Crashes* points out, these "surges in the credit supply appear to be becoming larger."[9]

Throughout these troublesome decades, the work of both Kindleberger and Hyman Minsky have received more attention. The relevance of Kindleberger's book continues to grow in the eyes of the financial community, and each succeeding edition has benefitted from more urgent, contemporary material to analyze and digest.[10]

Limitations

If *Manias, Panics, and Crashes* has one major limitation, it is its lack of ideas as to how future financial crises can be prevented. Kindleberger can be persuasive in dismissing popular remedies for reckless lending behavior; for example, he denies that increased regulation is the answer. Like other aspects of his argument, this stance is rooted in historical evidence; he reminds the reader that, "Although banks have been regulated for more than three hundred years, the universal response to failure or near failure of banks is that more regulation or more effective regulation is needed."[11] His position also rests on the idea that, because manias result from the excessively rapid growth of credit, there is no regulation that is suited to solving the problem;[12] such manic periods are intimately associated with the practice of capitalism*—which relies on the creation of credit in order to function. Any attempt to regulate the economy by limiting credit could sink the entire system into a permanent recession.

There is an obvious defeatism in this statement. Not all

regulation is equal, and while a new era may present new problems, it may also offer new solutions. The Nobel Prize*—winning economist Paul Krugman* has refuted Kindleberger's attitude towards regulation, arguing that new US banking regulations after the Great Depression* gave the country "a workable solution, involving both guarantees and oversight" and provided a half-century of financial stability.[13] Krugman passionately argues that such governance can be updated to today's needs, whereas Kindleberger's book stoically accepts reckless behavior. Kindleberger might be passionate about the need for a "lender of last resort"* to rescue a country from financial crisis (preventing a bad situation from becoming a full-on global disaster), but he seems resigned to the belief that serious economic crises are an inevitable aspect of the capitalist system.

1. Charles P. Kindleberger and Robert Z. Aliber, *Manias, Panics, and Crashes: A History of Financial Crises* (Basingstoke: Palgrave MacMillan, 2015),185.

2. Piero Pasotti and Alessandro Vercelli, "Kindleberger and Financial Crises," *Financialisation, Economy, Society, and Sustainable Development Working Paper Series* 104 (February, 2015), accessed March 22, 2016, http://fessud.eu/wp-content/uploads/2015/01/Kindleberger-and-Financial-Crises- Fessud-final_Working-Paper-104.pdf.

3. *Economist*, "Of Manias, Panics, and Crashes," July 19, 2003, accessed March 22, 2016, http://www.economist.com/node/1923462.

4. Ashoka Mody, "Germany must lead by example on fixing its banks," *Financial Times*, May 27, 2013, accessed March 22, 2016, http://www.ft.com/intl/cms/s/0/10e7ccbe-c46f-11e2-9ac0-00144feab7de.html#axzz43Y4Huy4b.

5. John Maudlin and Jonathan Tepper, *Code Red: How to Protect Your Savings From the Coming Crisis* (Hoboken: John Wiley & Sons, 2013), 193.

6. Kindleberger and Aliber, *Manias, Panics, and Crashes*, 1.

7. Kindleberger and Aliber, *Manias, Panics, and Crashes*, 5.

8. Nassim Nicholas Taleb, *The Black Swan: The Impact of the Highly Improbable* (London: Penguin, 2007), 43.

9. Kindleberger and Aliber, *Manias, Panics, and Crashes*, 16.

10. Two examples of Kindleberger's continued prominence: *Economist*, "Of Manias, Panics, and Crashes"; and Paul Krugman, "China Bites the Cherry," *New York Times*, August 12, 2015, accessed March 22, 2016, http://krugman.blogs.nytimes.com/2015/08/12/china-bites-the-cherry/?_r=0.

11. Kindleberger and Aliber, *Manias, Panics, and Crashes*, 239.

12. Kindleberger and Aliber, *Manias, Panics, and Crashes*, 239.

13. Paul Krugman, "Why We Regulate," *New York Times*, May 13, 2012, accessed March 22, 2016, http://www.nytimes.com/2012/05/14/opinion/ krugman-why-we-regulate.html.

MODULE 8
PLACE IN THE AUTHOR'S WORK

KEY POINTS

* Kindleberger's work demonstrates a long-standing engagement with financial crises* through a distinctly international perspective.

* His 1973 book *The World in Depression, 1929–1939* was published five years before *Manias, Panics, and Crashes*, and laid the foundations for the arguments he develops in the later book.

* While Kindleberger was already a highly esteemed economist, *Manias, Panics, and Crashes* solidified his reputation and legacy.

Positioning

Charles P. Kindleberger's *Manias, Panics, and Crashes: A History of Financial Crises* may build directly on the ideas of the US economist Hyman Minsky,* but it also advances his own earlier work.

In 1973, Kindleberger published *The World in Depression, 1929–1939*, which argued that the Great Depression* in the 1930s was wide, deep, and prolonged because there had been no international "lender of last resort"* to bail out failing financial institutions such as struggling banks.[1] The book was radical in that it departed from the US-centric perspective that had dominated the subject. As fellow economists have noted, "While much of the earlier literature, often authored by Americans, focused on the Great Depression in the US, Kindleberger emphasized that

127

the Depression had a prominent international and, in particular, European dimension."[2]

A "lender of last resort," Kindleberger argued, could have calmed the panic and crash that led to the Great Depression, but the world was at an awkward crossroads. Britain, the previous leader of the world economy, was too weak to fulfill this role after World War I* (1914–18) and America, the rising new leader of the world, was unwilling to assume such responsibility.[3] Consequently, the "negative feedback loop"*—vicious circle—of the global crash was allowed to get worse and worse, with no "lender of last resort" to put the brakes on an economic train wreck.

Kindleberger saw a strong parallel between this lack of American leadership in the 1930s and its lack of leadership in the 1970s, when the global system was faltering due to the collapse of the "gold standard"* and the Bretton Woods system.* These two mechanisms had, in Kindleberger's eyes, provided much-needed stability to the global economy—but in 1971 the United States abandoned the gold standard, which in turn led to the abandonment of the Bretton Woods system of foreign exchange. For Kindleberger, this sowed the seeds of future instability.[4] Given subsequent financial crises, it can easily be argued that he was right.

> "Kindleberger's argument grew out of his interpretation of the Great Depression."
>
> —— Lord Robert Skidelsky, afterword to *Manias, Panics, and Crashes: A History of Financial Crises*

Integration

Kindleberger's distinguished career began with an interest in foreign exchange. His first book, *International Short-Term Capital Movements* (1937), examined how capital*—financial resources—was being moved around the world by speculators* to earn higher interest rates. It also explored the international debts that were accumulated by changes in the international balance of payments* (whether a country was a "creditor" or "debtor" to the rest of the world).[5] *The Dollar Shortage* (1950) addressed the relationship between a country's level of economic development and its international balance of payments.[6]

This earlier focus on international trade perhaps explains the uniquely international perspective that Kindleberger brought to *The World in Depression, 1929–1939* and *Manias, Panics, and Crashes*. In this sense, his preoccupations with international capital movements and balance of payments remained consistent throughout his career, steadily expanding to a much wider view of economic and financial history. By the 1970s Kindleberger was focusing on the nature of financial crises, past and present, with a particular eye on panics, contagion,* and the need for an international "lender of last resort."

Significance

Manias, Panics, and Crashes was highly significant to Kindleberger's career and legacy. An esteemed economics* professor at the Massachusetts Institute of Technology (MIT),* his reputation was already secure thanks to his previous work and publications, most notably *The World in Depression, 1929–1939*. Praised by the famous Canadian-born economist John Kenneth Galbraith,* this book is a classic in its own right.[7]

With *Manias, Panics, and Crashes*, Kindleberger became regarded as a pioneer in his field. In 1978, he proclaimed the increased fragility of the new global economy due to the collapse of the US gold standard and international Bretton Woods system. It was just at this moment, in the late 1970s and early 1980s, that the full impact of this fragility would be felt within the global economy, and be sustained for the next 30-plus years. Between 1982 and 2007, the global economy would experience six of the ten biggest financial bubbles* in the history of markets.[8] Kindleberger's book "paved the way" in analyzing the sources of these crises, and in considering what can be done to minimize their impact on the global economic system.[9] His book came to rival, and probably surpass *The World in Depression* in both its achievement and popularity—although it is undoubtedly an extension of the ideas explored in that earlier study.

---

1. Charles P. Kindleberger and Robert Z. Aliber, *Manias, Panics, and Crashes: A History of Financial Crises* (Basingstoke: Palgrave MacMillan, 2015), 24.

2. Piero Pasotti and Alessandro Vercelli, "Kindleberger and Financial Crises," *Financialisation, Economy, Society, and Sustainable Development Working Paper Series* 104 (February, 2015), accessed March 22, 2016, http://fessud.eu/wp-content/uploads/2015/01/Kindleberger-and-Financial-Crises- Fessud-final_Working-Paper-104.pdf: 6.

3. Charles P. Kindleberger, *The World in Depression, 1929–1939* (Berkeley; Los Angeles: University of California Press, 1973), 292.

4. Kindleberger, *The World in Depression*, 308.

5. Charles P. Kindleberger, *International Short-Term Capital Movements* (New York: Columbia University Press, 1937).

6. Charles P. Kindleberger, *The Dollar Shortage* (New York: John Wiley & Sons, 1950).

7. Kindleberger, *The World in Depression, 1929–1939*, 1.

8. Kindleberger and Aliber, *Manias, Panics, and Crashes*, 18.

9. Sakis Gekas, "Different Because Worse," *Dublin Review of Books* 16 (Winter 2010), accessed March 22, 2016, http://www.drb.ie/essays/different- because-worse.

SECTION 3
IMPACT

MODULE 9
THE FIRST RESPONSES

KEY POINTS

* While Kindleberger appeals for an international "lender of last resort"* to bail out large financial institutions that are struggling, he does not specify what this entity should look like in reality.

* Subsequent financial crises* showed that such a "lender of last resort" was indeed needed, and these events were incorporated into new editions of *Manias, Panics, and Crashes*.

* Given that the world economy grew more volatile after the publication of *Manias, Panics, and Crashes*, more people became convinced of irrational investment behavior—and by Kindleberger's argument.

Criticism

Upon publication in 1978, *Manias, Panics, and Crashes: A History of Financial Crises* was generally praised by peer reviews, although flaws were also mentioned. One 1979 issue of the *Economic History Review* applauded the "immense weight of learning" that Charles P. Kindleberger had brought to such an "apparently wild" subject, and said that it yielded new insights.[1] But the review also questioned the book's conclusion, criticizing Kindleberger's emphasis on the need for an international "lender of last resort," without explaining what form it should take.[2]

The *Economic Journal* also lauded the balance that Kindleberger achieved between scholarliness and style, but was unconvinced by his basic assumption that the "euphoric" periods of a mania reflected "irrational" behavior on the part of investors* and institutions.[3] This early review maintained that this behavior is compatible with market efficiency,* and so sided with the efficient market hypothesis* that was in vogue at the time (and at odds with Kindleberger's ideas).[4] The reviewer also found Kindleberger's enthusiasm for a "lender of last resort" to be "vague," and disparaged his "literary economics," referring to the work's accessible narrative writing style.[5]

> "Kindleberger's enthusiasm for lenders of last resort is vague."
>
> —— Patrick Minford, "Manias, Panics, and Crashes. A History of Financial Crises. By Charles P. Kindleberger," Economic Journal

Responses

When Kindleberger wrote *Manias, Panics, and Crashes*, the academic environment was largely loyal to the efficient market hypothesis and its assumption that investors' behavior tends to be rational. Given his observation that it is in fact far from rational, Kindleberger issued a major challenge to orthodox thinking in his field. He persisted with his argument through several subsequent, revised editions of his book, and eventually the critics caught up with its conclusions.

Reviewers of the first edition of *Manias, Panics, and Crashes* noticed that most of Kindleberger's (many) examples of past financial crises came from the period 1719–1929, "with some reference to more recent events."[6] However, with the financial crisis of 1982,* a new era of economic turbulence and fragility began. Kindleberger and, after his death in 2003, his successor Robert Z. Aliber* responded with six new editions of *Manias, Panics, and Crashes* from 1989 to 2015. Each of these editions had a wealth of new material to draw on, analyze, and compare. For example, the 1996 edition included analyses of the US stock market crash of 1987* ("Black Monday," when nervousness in the markets following a short conflict between the United States and Iran saw a plunge in the value of shares) and the 1995 peso devaluation* (following the Mexican government's decision to devalue the peso against the US dollar by 15 percent, investors sought to sell their investments in Mexico; the consequence was a crisis that spread to the Asian markets). The 2000 edition included an examination of the 1997 East Asian crisis,* which began in Thailand and then spread quickly to other East Asian countries. None of the new case studies stand alone; they each become part of the larger argument about financial crises, the "biologic regularity"* (a set of consistent stages of development) they all share, and what can be done about them.

It was not long before Kindleberger's appeal for an international "lender of last resort" also found more support. The political scientist Robert Keohane* developed the thesis and rebranded it "the theory of hegemonic* stability"—a label that stuck over time[7] ("hegemonic" here refers to the dominance of a political or economic superpower). Keohane himself noticed a growing literature centered on this topic and surveyed it in his book *After*

Hegemony: Cooperation and Discord in the World of Political Economy (1984).[8] A new conversation had begun.

Conflict and Consensus

As time passed, *Manias, Panics, and Crashes* became regarded as a "classic" by most of the academic and financial community.[9] Even while admiring Kindleberger's study, however, such critics still take issue with central aspects of it, such as its failure to define "financial crises."[10] While Kindleberger himself admitted that this key term might be beyond any sort of precise and generally agreed clarification, critics have insisted on its absolute necessity.[11] Likewise, the book says little about the distinction between crises that have led to depressions and those that have not.[12]

Beyond such disputes over the actual content of the book, large theoretical challenges also remain. The efficient market hypothesis has not gone away, and its greatest publicist—the economist and author Burton G. Malkiel*— extols its virtues in his recent best selling book *A Random Walk Down Wall Street* (the latest edition of which was also published in 2015). In Malkiel's eyes, in a "mania" investors will realize sooner or later the true value of their assets,* and act accordingly— that is to say, rationally: "While the stock market in the short run may be a voting mechanism, in the long run it is a weighing mechanism. True value will win out in the end."[13] Kindleberger and his successor and updater, Aliber, do not have much time for any form of the efficient market hypothesis; according to Aliber's 2015 edition, the EMH implies "clairvoyance" on the part of investors.[14]

1. W. Ashworth, *"Manias, Panics, and Crashes: A History of Financial Crises* by Charles P. Kindleberger," *Economic History Review* 32, no. 3 (1979): 421–2.

2. Ashworth, *"Manias, Panics, and Crashes,"* 422.

3. Patrick Minford, *"Manias, Panics, and Crashes: A History of Financial Crises* by Charles P. Kindleberger," *Economic Journal* 89 (December, 1979): 947.

4. Minford, *"Manias, Panics, and Crashes,"* 947.

5. Minford, *"Manias, Panics, and Crashes,"* 947, 948.

6. Ashworth, *"Manias, Panics, and Crashes,"* 421.

7. Stephen Meardon, "On Kindleberger and Hegemony: From Berlin to M.I.T. and Back," *Bowdoin Digital Commons*, September 29, 2013, accessed March 22, 2016, http://digitalcommons.bowdoin. edu/cgi/viewcontent. cgi?article=1003&context=econpapers.

8. Meardon, "On Kindleberger and Hegemony."

9. See Christopher Kobrak and Mira Wilkins, *History and Financial Crisis: Lessons from the 20th Century* (New York: Routledge, 2013), 3. For an example from the financial community, see Jason Zweig, "Read It and Reap: The Best Books for Investors," *Wall Street Journal*, November 28, 2014, accessed March 22, 2016, http://www.wsj.com/articles/read-it-and-reap-the-best-books-for-investors-1417213387.

10. Kobrak and Wilkins, *History and Financial Crises*, 3.

11. Kobrak and Wilkins, *History and Financial Crises*, 4.

12. Richard Sylla, "Financial Disturbances and Depressions: The View from Economic History," Social Science Research Network: Levy Economics Institute Working Paper 47 (April 1991): 3.

13. Burton G. Malkiel, "The Efficient Market Hypothesis and Its Critics," *Journal of Economic Perspectives* 17, no. 1 (2003): 61.

14. Charles P. Kindleberger and Robert Z. Aliber, *Manias, Panics, and Crashes: A History of Financial Crises* (Basingstoke: Palgrave MacMillan, 2015), 53—6.

MODULE 10
THE EVOLVING DEBATE

KEY POINTS

* As financial crises* mounted over time, Kindleberger's ideas, particularly his call for an international "lender of last resort"* capable of bailing out large financial institutions that find themselves in trouble were taken more seriously.

* A general theory of "hegemonic* stability"—a stability founded on the dominance of a single nation—evolved to address what such a "lender of last resort" would look like.

* Since the publication of *Manias, Panics, Crashes*, the discipline of economics* has embraced the study of irrational investment behavior through new fields like behavioral economics,* which draws on the field of psychology*—the study of the mind and behavior—to explain economic decision-making.

Uses and Problems

Charles P. Kindleberger's view of financial crises in *Manias, Panics, and Crashes: A History of Financial Crises* ultimately calls for serious policy coordination at a global level. That said, and as critics of Kindleberger have noted, his vision of what an international "lender of last resort" should look like in real life can sometimes seem vague.

From the 1980s onward economists and political scientists, inspired by Kindleberger's ideas, began to meet the challenge of designing such an entity. The US political scientist Robert Keohane* began to envision a real-life, international "lender of last resort" in his book *After Hegemony: Cooperation and Discord* *in the World of Political Economy* (1984).[1] The distinguished economist Barry Eichengreen* wrote "Hegemonic Stability Theories of the International Monetary System" in 1987, in which he examined the conditions, institutions, and degree of leadership necessary to achieve international monetary coordination.[2] This issue would become an abiding interest for Eichengreen, while Robert Gilpin,* a scholar of economic relations on the international scale, published *The Political Economy of International Relations* (1987), influenced by Kindleberger's position. This book examined America's leadership in the global financial structure after World War II* and how it had since declined. For Gilpin, the US is absolutely central to the creation of international financial cooperation.[3] These, and many other such studies inspired by Kindleberger, demonstrate how his insights have been used. Thinkers influenced by Kindleberger recognize that financial crises are international in nature, and tend to conclude that stabilizing them calls for new international cooperation. Achieving this is an ongoing challenge— perhaps made even more difficult in the current age of growing economic nationalism*—an ideology in which a nation considers its own economic health to be entirely, and uncompromisingly, paramount at the expense of the global economy's overall health.

> *"Innovations that have transformed finance over the past decade have substantially improved the overall stability and resilience of the US financial system. But these improvements are unlikely to have brought an end to what Charles Kindleberger called 'manias and panics.'"*
>
> ——Timothy F. Geithner, "Change and Challenges Facing the US Financial System," *BIS Review*

Schools of Thought

Manias, Panics, and Crashes was first published during the heyday of the efficient market hypothesis,* with its assumption that investors* behave rationally. The book directly diverged from the dominant way of thinking about the nature of the economic cycles that lead to catastrophes. When the world experienced a series of financial crises, starting with that of 1982,* Kindleberger's work suddenly seemed spot on: a new recognition of bubbles* and irrational investment behavior turned the established way of thinking on its head.[4] Behavioral economics, for example, is a rapidly evolving field that emerged through this period: it holds that investors are generally far from rational, and instead reflect psychological biases such as overconfidence, prejudiced judgments, and herd mentality. Like Kindleberger, behavioral economists believe (and worry) that such behavior makes bubbles self-fulfilling, in the sense that when everyone thinks asset* prices will rise, they buy assets, thereby causing the prices to rise; when everyone thinks prices are going to fall, they sell, and prices tumble.[5]

Academics exploring how an international "lender of last resort" could work politically form a broader school of thought. They are engaged in an ongoing debate that includes many politicians as well, often working on strategies to solve real-life crises. In his memoir, for example, former US treasury secretary Timothy Geithner* recalls warning investment banks against complacency in 2004, quoting from *Manias, Panics, and Crashes,* and says that the book deeply influenced his own views on financial crises.[6]

In Current Scholarship

Since Kindleberger's death in 2003, the economist Robert Z. Aliber* has edited and updated subsequent editions of *Manias, Panics, and Crashes.* In this role he now shares ownership and development of the book's project, adding new examples of financial crises and irrational behavior to its already vast panorama.

In the seventh, and to date the most recent, edition, Aliber takes the book's argument one step further in an inventive turn of his own. He examines a sequence of financial crises that have taken place one after the other over the past 40 years—first the Mexico and South American financial crisis of the early 1980s,* then the Japanese crash of 1990,* then the East Asian crisis* of 1997, and finally the real estate crashes affecting several countries in 2007 and 2008.* He argues that these successive "waves" of credit-fueled booms and busts* were causally related.[7] When the international money feeding one mania suddenly fled the country and panic set in, most of this money was moved to another international location to begin pumping up another (ill-fated) boom.[8] Aliber's point is that roughly the same international money, sloshing around the world and guided by institutions such as large global banks,was behind each of these booms and the consequent busts. This is a bold, highly specific argument in the spirit of Kindleberger's original thesis.

Beyond Aliber's scholarly development of Kindleberger's

argument, discussion of it is widespread throughout the worlds of academia, finance, politics, and journalism. The work enjoys high esteem in the business world as well; one private business advisory group even profiles the book on its website, proclaiming that it should be "a regular staple for all, from central bankers to ordinary bankers, from investors to regular businessmen and women, in the halls of government and in the average living room."[9] Kindleberger's ideas are now widely accepted in multiple spheres, and are praised for their precision, foresight, and continuing relevance worldwide.

---

1. Robert Keohane, *After Hegemony: Cooperation and Discord in the World of Political Economy* (Princeton: Princeton University Press, 1984).

2. Eichengreen, Barry, "Hegemonic Stability Theories of the International Monetary System," in *Can Nations Agree? Issues in International Economic Cooperation* by Richard Cooper et al, (Washington, DC: Brookings Institution, 1989): 255–98.

3. Robert Gilpin, *The Political Economy of International Relations* (Princeton: Princeton University Press, 1987).

4. *Economist*, "Of Manias, Panics, and Crashes," July 19, 2003, accessed March 22, 2016, http://www.economist.com/node/1923462.

5. Todd A. Knoop, *Business Cycle Economics: Understanding Recessions and Depressions from Boom to Bust* (Santa Barbara, CA: Praeger, 2015), 172.

6. Timothy F. Geithner, *Stress Test: Reflections on Financial Crises* (New York: Crown Publishers, 2014).

7. Charles P. Kindleberger and Robert Z. Aliber, *Manias, Panics, and Crashes: A History of Financial Crises* (Basingstoke: Palgrave MacMillan, 2015), ix.

8. Kindleberger and Aliber, *Manias, Panics, and Crashes*, ix.

9. Gail Fosler, "Lessons from Kindleberger on the Financial Crisis," The Gail Fosler Group, April 28, 2013, accessed March 22, 2016, http://www. gailfosler.com/lessons-from-kindleberger-on-the-financial-crisis.

MODULE 11
IMPACT AND INFLUENCE TODAY

KEY POINTS

- *Manias, Panics, and Crashes* remains a popular classic in economics.

- The question as to how to contain financial crises* is still a challenge to today's economists and policymakers.

- Whether fixed exchange rates* are part of the solution is still a subject of debate.

Position

Charles P. Kindleberger's *Manias, Panics, and Crashes: A History of Financial Crises* remains influential and relevant more than 40 years after it was first published in 1978. It is still frequently mentioned in relation to current events—for example, when the Chinese stock market crashed in the summer of 2015, the British economic journal the *Economist* opened a feature on this news with a direct link to Kindleberger's framework: "The great Charles Kindleberger described the pattern of how bubbles form and then burst in his book *Manias, Panics and Crashes*."[1]

Kindleberger's appeals have clearly been heard at the highest possible levels of political economy. In the foreword to *Manias, Panics, and Crashes*, the US economist Robert M. Solow* remarks that Kindleberger "would certainly have been fascinated—and probably gratified—by the way the Federal Reserve* acted during the [2008] crisis not only as lender of last resort* to the banking system but almost as lender of last resort to the whole economy."[2]

Furthermore, in the 40th anniversary edition of Kindleberger's earlier book, *The World in Depression, 1929–1939*, its editors note the continuing importance of his "theory of hegemonic* stability" during a period of global financial crisis and US political dysfunction.[3] The publisher's description of the book highlights its use by major players in global economic politics: "This masterpiece of economic history shows why US treasury secretary Lawrence Summers,* during the darkest hours of the 2008 Global Financial Crisis,* turned to Kindleberger and his peers for guidance."[4]

> "The most rigorous—and certainly the greatest—book of its kind, Charles Kindleberger's definitive **Manias, Panics and Crashes.**"
>
> —— Nick Murray, "A Treasure Trove of Financial Folly,"
> *Financial Advisor*

Interaction

Countries can still choose whether to have fixed or free-floating currencies.* While Kindleberger sees fixed exchange rates as more stable, this has been seriously challenged by the International Monetary Fund's* research, which discovered no empirical differences in volatility between the two systems.[5] The International Monetary Fund (IMF) is an institution founded to secure international financial stability and cooperation; it commonly lends money to nations in financial distress in return for structural changes to their economies such as the implementation of spending cuts or the privatization of state-owned businesses.

The debate over who is to blame for the financial crisis of 2008* also continues, with Lehman Brothers* (the New York-based investment bank that went bankrupt in 2008) often cast as the scapegoat. Kindleberger would see Lehman Brothers as a small player in a much larger dynamic: one in which the supply of credit was surging across the board, and investors* were entering a "euphoric" phase of irrationally optimistic forecasts.[6]

More generally, the basic premise of *Manias, Panics, and Crashes*—that there is a "biologic regularity"* to financial crises that has been consistent throughout history, with oversupply of credit being the primary issue—has been refuted by a vast number of critics still analyzing the 2008 crash. Many of them see the crash as having been a totally unique product of its time, with little in common with other financial crises from history.

The Continuing Debate

In his later career, Kindleberger consistently saw the end of the US gold standard* and the mechanisms of financial relations between nations that defined the Bretton Woods system* in the early 1970s, and conversion of the dollar and many other currencies to a free-floating arrangement, as a new source of global economic instability. A 2004 paper from the International Monetary Fund directly challenged this view. It found that in the 30 preceding years, the volatility of fixed exchange rates was about the same as that of floating rates—something that is possible because a currency pegged to the US dollar must still go up and down with the US dollar against the world's other (non-pegged) currencies.[7]

More than this, the study showed that a volatile currency had very little effect on international trade flows going in and out of a country.[8] This means that a fixed exchange rate system may not provide the kind of stability Kindleberger envisioned.

Many prominent thinkers and writers continue to ignore Kindleberger's insights when analyzing the crash of 2008. Lehman Brothers is still often cast as the source of the crisis: popular books have been published with titles such as *A Colossal Failure of Common Sense: The Inside Story of the Collapse of Lehman Brothers* (2009) by the bank's former vice-chairman Lawrence G. McDonald* and the economist Patrick Robinson; and the journalist Vicky Ward's* *The Devil's Casino: Friendship, Betrayal, and the High Stakes Games Played Inside Lehman Brothers* (2010).[9]

Other causes have been pinpointed as the "true" source of the crisis by thinkers who see these factors as completely unique to 2008. Financial journalist Scott Patterson's book *The Quants* (2010) argues that Wall Street's math-minded "quantitative analysts" took over much of the financial system in the year preceding the crash, and were responsible for it.[10] One trader from this era was bold enough to publish the book *How I Caused the Credit Crunch* (2009), implying that he was solely responsible.[11] None of these books view the crash from Kindleberger's much wider, historic perspective.

1. Buttonwood, "China's Stockmarket: The Great Leap Backward," *Economist*, July 8, 2015, accessed March 22, 2016, http://www.economist.com/blogs/ buttonwood/2015/07/chinas-stockmarket.

2. Charles P. Kindleberger and Robert Z. Aliber, *Manias, Panics, and Crashes: A History of Financial Crises* (Basingstoke: Palgrave MacMillan, 2015), viii.

3. Charles P. Kindleberger, *The World in Depression, 1929–1939*, ed. J. Bradford DeLong and Barry Eichengreen (Berkeley; Los Angeles: University of California Press, 2013), ix.

4. University of California Press, "*The World in Depression, 1929–1939*," accessed March 22, 2016, http://www.ucpress.edu/book. php?isbn=9780520275850.

5. Peter Clark, et al., "Exchange Rate Volatility and Trade Flows—Some New Evidence," International Monetary Fund (May 2004): 54–5, accessed March 21, 2016, https://www.imf.org/external/np/res/exrate/2004/eng/051904. pdf.

6. Kindleberger and Aliber, *Manias, Panic, and Crashes,* 15.

7. Clark et al., "Exchange Rate Volatility," 54–5.

8. Clark et al., "Exchange Rate Volatility," 55.

9. Lawrence G. McDonald with Patrick Robinson, *A Colossal Failure of Common Sense: The Inside Story of the Collapse of Lehman Brothers* (New York: Three Rivers Press, 2009); Vicky Ward, *The Devil's Casino: Friendship, Betrayal, and the High-Stakes Games Played Inside Lehman Brothers* (Hoboken: John Wiley & Sons, 2010).

10. Scott Patterson, *The Quants: How a New Breed of Math Whizzes Conquered Wall Street and Nearly Destroyed It* (New York: Crown Business, 2010).

11. Tetsuya Ishikawa, *How I Caused the Credit Crunch: An Insider's Story of the Financial Meltdown* (London: Icon Books, 2009).

MODULE 12
WHERE NEXT?

KEY POINTS

* Kindleberger's text looks set to remain a touchstone for economists and politicians seeking to stabilize the world economy.

* *Manias, Panics, and Crashes* is an evolving text that illustrates exactly how financial crises* work, and that provides an arena for possible solutions to global economic upheaval.

* *Manias, Panics, and Crashes* explains the cycle of boom and bust* in a way that is historically grounded, of the moment, and enduringly human.

Potential

In today's contexts, the importance and influence of Charles P. Kindleberger's work looks set to endure, especially since these contexts so closely (and frighteningly) mirror the concerns that *Manias, Panics, and Crashes: A History of Financial Crises* foreshadowed in the 1970s. For example, the Chinese stock market crashed on June 12, 2015 with the value of the Shanghai stock exchange sinking by a third.[1] After a period of stabilization, the same market crashed again at the start of 2016 and triggered a global retreat of stock markets.[2] Meanwhile, the bubble* in oil prices also burst, incurring huge deflationary* pressures on the world economy—a rise in the value of money, experienced as a fall in prices.

All of this was big news, and Kindleberger's text was one of the most frequently mentioned by its commentators. Regarding China's 2015 stock market crash, two distinguished professors from the University of Hong Kong stated that "Though the blame game is ongoing, the historian Charles Kindleberger's 1978 book *Manias, Panics, and Crashes: A History of Financial Crises* offers the perfect explanation of what China is experiencing."[3] Speaking about the collapse in oil prices, one commentator writes that "the energy cycle fits the classic scenario that Professor Kindleberger described in his classic history of financial manias, *Manias, Panics, and Crashes*."[4] These examples reflect just a snippet of Kindleberger's enduring presence in contemporary conversations about the most significant global economic events. If anything, the book continues to gain relevance over time.

> "China's problem is much like that of Japan's in the early 1990s; the amount that households wish to save is much larger than business firms can profitably invest."
> —— Robert Z. Aliber, *Manias, Panics, and Crashes: A History of Financial Crises*

Future Directions

New editions of *Manias, Panics, and Crashes* have continued to be issued since Kindleberger's death in 2003, including much new material and analysis; his argument continues to evolve. The book's current coauthor and editor, University of Chicago professor Robert Z. Aliber,* added an epilogue to the 2015 edition that focuses on China, warning that its high rates of growth are actually a bubble ready to burst, especially as so much of the country's growth has been built on credit. The events of early 2016, with the Chinese stock market falling steeply and prompting a global sell-off of shares, could be viewed as this shift from the "manic" stage of Kindleberger's cycle to the "panic." One American academic has said that, given these events in China,"the need for an eighth edition of *Manias, Panics, and Crashes* may soon be apparent."[5] Aliber has picked up the baton from Kindleberger; the discussion that *Manias, Panics, and Crashes* began in 1978 rages on in ever wider circles and—given the state of the global economy—with increasing urgency.

Kindleberger's central recommendation to soothe volatile (unstable) markets is the establishment of an international "lender of last resort."* Although a global financial institution existed when Kindleberger first formulated his position, he was not convinced that it could sufficiently fill the "institutional vacuum" he identified. The International Monetary Fund* (IMF) was established in the 1940s to act as such an international "lender of last resort."[6] However, many economists question how effective it is, asking "whether the presence of the IMF as a supplier of national currencies to countries with financial crises encouraged profligate national financial policies."[7]

Ultimately, the IMF or any international "lender of last resort" must pull off a difficult balancing act: it must be there and ready to lend in the case of financial crises, but it must always make the delivery of such help uncertain, so that its presence does not encourage reckless behavior.[8] The most recent edition of *Manias,*

Panics, and Crashes includes a "report card on the IMF as an international lender of last resort," with a fairly damning verdict: "The Fund has lost sight of its original mandate to manage the international monetary system," and does not adequately recognize the dangers that huge cross-border investment flows* pose to the global economy.[9] The installation of a proper "lender of last resort" seems to be an ongoing project.

Summary

While it does borrow heavily from the ideas of the economist Hyman Minsky,* Kindleberger's *Manias, Panics, and Crashes* was a truly pioneering study that has stood the test of time. If anything, it has grown increasingly relevant to the most pressing, high-stakes questions facing today's economy. The book was published in 1978, when highly rational and mathematical models of efficiency* were all the rage in economics* departments. Rather than follow this trend, *Manias, Panics, and Crashes* provided a novel perspective on how markets work, and one that proved prophetic. Kindleberger used a "literary economics," employing an enjoyable, narrative style to argue that not only is the international economy inherently unstable (due to surges in credit, as Minsky had argued before him in a domestic context), but that the collapse of the US gold standard* and Bretton Woods system* in the 1970s was making it more prone to crisis.

While looking at economic history in an innovative, unorthodox way, the framework Kindleberger developed ultimately anticipated the future. Much more than that, he diagnosed this enduring cycle of mania-panic-crash as a function of credit surges (and, as Aliber later added through further analysis, cross-border investment flows). This conclusion is still debatable, but Kindleberger's detailed and historically substantiated description of the stages of these cycles sheds light on today's global economic events in compelling ways—and makes the ambition of achieving greater international economic stability seem possible. In pursuing this vital aim, *Manias, Panics, and Crashes* remains essential reading.

---

1. Katie Allen, "Why is China's Stock Market in Crisis?" *Guardian*, July 8, 2015, accessed March 22, 2016, http://www.theguardian.com/business/2015/jul/08/china-stock-market-crisis-explained.

2. Will Hutton, "Why Are We Looking on Helplessly as Markets Crash All Over the World?" *Guardian*, January 17, 2016, accessed March 22, 2016, http://www.theguardian.com/commentisfree/2016/jan/17/china-economic-crisis-world-economy-global-capitalism.

3. Andrew Sheng and Xiao Geng, "China's Live Stress Test," Project Syndicate: The World's Opinion Page, July 21, 2015, accessed March 22, 2016, http://www.project-syndicate.org/commentary/china-stock-market-government-intervention-by-andrew-sheng-and-xiao-geng-2015-07?barrier=true.

4. Michael Lewitt, "Oil is Going to Fall by 50%... Again," Michael Lewitt's Sure Money, September 28, 2015, accessed March 22, 2016, http://suremoneyinvestor.com/2015/09/oil-is-going-to-fall-by-50-again/.

5. Joseph P. Joyce, "The Enduring Relevance of 'Manias, Panics, and Crashes.'" Capital Ebbs and Flows, December 14, 2015, accessed March 22, 2016, https://blogs.wellesley.edu/jjoyce/2015/12/14/the-enduring-relevance-of-manias-panics-and-crashes-2/.

6. Charles P. Kindleberger and Robert Z. Aliber, *Manias, Panics, and Crashes: A History of Financial Crises* (Basingstoke: Palgrave MacMillan, 2015), 35.

7. Kindleberger and Aliber, *Manias, Panics, and Crashes*, 35.

8. Kindleberger and Aliber, *Manias, Panics, and Crashes*, 35.

9. Kindleberger and Aliber, *Manias, Panics, and Crashes*, 310–12.

GLOSSARY OF TERMS

1. **Asset:** a resource or piece of property owned by someone or something, which possesses an economic value.

2. **Bagehot doctrine:** in his 1873 book *Lombard Street*, the British businessman and writer Walter Bagehot urged the Bank of England to calm financial panics by lending freely to distressed but solvent banks at a penalty interest rate. This policy became popular among central banks, and was subsequently known as the "Bagehot doctrine."

3. **Balance of payments:** a term that describes whether a nation is a creditor or a debtor to the rest of the world.

4. **Behavioral economics:** a relatively new field of economics that studies the decision-making processes of individuals and institutions, in an attempt to correct assumptions about their "rational" behavior. The psychological, emotional, and quite irrational aspects of market participants are emphasized in this field.

5. **Behavioral finance:** a field of finance exploring the psychological characteristics of market participants to explain market movements and, in particular, irrational systematic errors.

6. **Biologic regularity:** a term Kindleberger employs to argue that all financial crises share the same stages and underlying dynamic of boom and bust.

7. **Boom and bust:** an economic cycle in which a period of rapid growth and prosperity is suddenly followed by one of sharp economic collapse.

8. **Bretton Woods system:** an elaborate postwar agreement between numerous Western countries, establishing monetary arrangements between them as well as other financial relations. It operated from 1945 until the United States abandoned the gold standard in 1971.

9. **Bubble:** when the price of an asset, security, or commodity increases significantly in a way that cannot be explained by economic fundamentals.

10. **Capital:** financial resources, like cash or the value of other assets, available for use by their owner.

11. **Capitalism:** an economic system in which the means of production are privately owned and used in the pursuit of profit. The production of goods and services is

based on the laws of supply and demand.

12. **Central bank:** a government institution designed to manage the country's interest rate and money supply, among other currency issues.

13. **Classical economics:** a movement of the late eighteenth and early nineteenth centuries, largely advocating the creation of free markets.

14. **Contagion:** the spread of market disturbances, which can occur regionally, nationally, or internationally. A contagion can either be an economic boom or a crisis that crosses national boundaries.

15. **Credit crunch:** an economic situation in which loans or other forms of investment capital are suddenly hard to obtain.

16. **Cross-border investment flows:** financial arrangements that cross national borders and typically take the form of loans, acquisitions, or credit.

17. **Currency crisis:** a crisis brought on by a fall in the value of a country's currency, which creates instability in its exchange rates with other currencies. This decrease in value and instability can scare off investors. It can also make it difficult for a country to maintain a fixed exchange rate.

18. **Default:** the failure to pay a loan or interest on a loan when it is due.

19. **Deflation:** a rise in the value of money, and, therefore, a fall in the value of prices.

20. **Displacement:** when a significant event like a war, or new policy like deregulation, leads to a sudden boom. Sometimes a displacement occurs when a new technology or innovation radically improves profitability in a market, like the boom in the technological information market of the late 1990s that followed the invention of the Internet.

21. **Dot.com boom:** a huge growth in stock prices experienced by industrialized countries in the late 1990s, driven by the growth of technology firms.

22. **East Asian crisis:** the 1997 financial crisis that started in Thailand and spread quickly to other East Asian countries.

23. **Economic history:** the study of economic phenomena of the past.

24. **Economic nationalism:** an ideology in which a nation considers its own economic health to be entirely, and uncompromisingly, paramount at the expense of the global economy's overall health.

25. **Economics:** the social science that seeks to describe the production, distribution, and consumption of scarce resources in a world of unlimited wants.

26. **Efficiency:** in economics, efficiency is a state in which all resources are optimally allocated—that is, they serve in the best way while minimizing waste.

27. **Efficient market hypothesis (EMH):** the idea that asset prices, including stock prices, capture all available information about that asset or respective company.

28. **Federal Reserve:** the central bank of the United States, which regulates the nation's monetary and financial systems.

29. **Financial crisis:** a broad term applied to various circumstances in which there is a sudden and significant fall in the price of a financial asset or assets.

30. **Financial crisis of 1982:** a prolonged crisis when many Latin American countries became unable to service their foreign debt, particularly to US banks, which spread the crisis abroad. The crisis was sparked in the summer of 1982, when Mexico's finance minister informed the US Federal Reserve that Mexico would no longer be able to service its $80 billion in foreign debt. Other South American countries soon followed suit.

31. **Financial crisis of 2008:** the worst financial crisis since the Great Depression, featuring widespread bank bailouts, stock market collapses, and housing market busts.

32. **Financial instability hypothesis:** an idea developed by the US economist Hyman Minsky, arguing that economic prosperity leads to reckless investment behavior, fueled by credit.

33. **Financial regulation:** the supervision of financial institutions, typically by government agencies and through prescribed requirements and guidelines.

34. **Fixed exchange rates:** when a currency's value is pegged to the value of another currency, or to a basket of currencies, by the government. Sometimes an exchange rate is fixed by declaring it to be worth a certain quantity of gold.

35. **Free-floating exchange rates:** when a currency is not fixed by its government, but instead allowed to fluctuate on the global currency markets.

36. **Global economy:** the interdependence of national economies around the world in trade and industry, functioning as one economic system.

37. **Gold standard:** when a country declares that its currency is worth a certain amount of gold, thereby fixing the value of the currency.

38. **Great Depression:** an extremely long and deep economic depression that began in 1929 and lasted until World War II.

39. **Hegemony:** a predominant position of leadership, or a predominant sphere of influence, held by one country over others.

40. **Inflation:** a fall in the value of money, and a rise in prices. This is often brought on by an increase in the money supply.

41. **Interest rates:** the price of borrowing, typically expressed as an annual percentage of the loan outstanding.

42. **International balance of payments:** the statement of a nation's economic transactions with the rest of the world. Each country tends to be a persistent "debtor" or "creditor" nation.

43. **International Monetary Fund (IMF):** an institution, based in the United States, founded to secure international financial stability and cooperation; it commonly lends money to nations in financial distress in return for structural changes to their economies, such as spending cuts and the privatization of state-owned businesses and assets.

44. **International propagation:** an idea developed by Kindleberger, which held that due to the interdependence of the global economy, financial crises can spread from one country to another, as if through "contagion."

45. **Investor:** a person who provides capital in the hope of gaining a financial return in the future. Such capital can be provided in the form of equity, debt securities, real estate, commodities, and so on.

46. **Japanese credit crisis:** a major financial crisis in Japan in the 1980s, which saw a boom-and-bust scenario in stocks and real estate.

47. **Lehman Brothers:** a large international investment bank that went bankrupt in September 2008, triggering a worldwide financial crisis.

48. **Lender of last resort:** a central bank that loans money to other banks or similar financial institutions that are nearing insolvency and collapse.

49. **Marshall Plan:** officially known as the European Recovery Program, the Marshall Plan was a post-World War II economic support package provided to Western Europe by the United States. It was worth $13 billion.

50. **Minsky Model:** the economist Hyman Minsky's model of the credit cycle, which Kindleberger developed further. The model has five stages: displacement, boom, euphoria, profit-taking, and panic.

51. **Monetarism:** a school of thought within economics based on the belief that an economy's performance is most strongly influenced by changes in the money supply.

52. **Nationalism:** is an extreme form of patriotism, which typically includes the belief that the interests of one's own nation-state are superior to those of other countries.

53. **Negative feedback loop:** when the disruption from an established norm creates a response that amplifies the negative change.

54. **Nobel Prize:** a set of international awards given every year to recognize outstanding academic, cultural, or scientific achievements.

55. **Payment imbalance:** when a nation exports more than it imports, or vice versa.

56. **Peso devaluation:** in December 1994, the Mexican government devalued its peso against the US dollar by almost 15 percent. Among the unexpected consequences was a mass sell-off of Mexican assets by international investors wanting to remove their money from the country. This prompted a financial crisis that soon spread to Asia and other parts of Latin America.

57. **Positive feedback loops:** when the disruption from an established norm creates a response that amplifies the positive change.

58. **Pro-cyclical:** expresses the idea that credit cycles are self-perpetuating. So

increases in the supply of credit prolong the expansion of a boom, and decreases in the supply of credit intensify the subsequent crash.

59. **Psychology:** the study of the human mind and behavior.

60. **Securities:** a financial agreement signifying ownership in a public-traded corporation (like a stock), a creditor relationship (bond) or right to ownership (option).

61. **South Sea bubble:** one of the greatest financial bubbles in history, associated with the collapse in value of shares in the South Sea Company—a British public-private company founded in 1711 that was granted a monopoly to trade with South America. Prices of shares in the company rose to astronomical heights before crashing dramatically in 1720.

62. **Speculator:** someone who invests in a financial asset hoping for a short-term gain over the next few days or weeks.

63. **State Department:** the US federal government's ministry for dealing with America's international relations.

64. **Stock:** a security that provides a share of ownership in a corporation, and so a claim on future assets and earnings of that business.

65. **Stock market crash of 1987:** also known as "Black Monday," this was a crash that occurred on 19 October, 1987, occasioned by tension in the Persian Gulf, when the Dow Jones Industrial Average fell over 20 percent. Other stock markets around the world experienced huge losses on the same date.

66. **Trade surplus:** when a country exports more to the rest of the world than it imports.

67. **World War I:** also known as the Great War, this was a global war from 1914 to 1918 which took place between the "Allies" (Great Britain, France, the Russian Empire, and the United States), and the "Central Powers" of Germany and Austro-Hungary.

68. **World War II:** a global war lasting 1939–45, primarily between the "Allies" (which included the United States, Soviet Union, China, Great Britain, and France), and the "Axis" powers of Germany, Italy, and Japan.

PEOPLE MENTIONED IN THE TEXT

1. **Robert Z. Aliber (b. 1930)** is a professor emeritus of economics at the University of Chicago. His primary subject has been the nature of foreign direct investment. Since Kindleberger's death, Aliber has edited and updated *Manias, Panics, and Crashes* through its last three editions.

2. **Walter Bagehot (1826–77)** was a British businessman, journalist, and political commentator. He wrote extensively about economics and the nature of financial crisis.

3. **Gordon Brown (b. 1951)** was prime minister of the United Kingdom from 2007 to 2010, and chancellor of the exchequer from 1997 to 2007.

4. **Michel Chevalier (1806–79)** was a French economist and statesman who commentated extensively on the nature of markets and market instability.

5. **Charles Darwin (1809–82)** was an English naturalist and scientist, best known for his book *The Origin of Species* (1859), the text on which modern evolutionary theory is largely founded.

6. **Barry Eichengreen (b. 1952)** is an American economist and academic.

7. **Eugene F. Fama (b. 1939)** is a Nobel Prize-winning economist whose primary subject has been the analysis of stock market behavior. He is credited with making the efficient market hypothesis credible through empirical evidence.

8. **Milton Friedman (1912–2006)** was a professor in economics and political science at the University of California, Berkeley. His work looks at the international monetary and financial system.

9. **John Kenneth Galbraith (1908–2006)** was a distinguished economist and public intellectual who taught at Harvard for over 50 years.

10. **Timothy F. Geithner (b. 1961)** is a former economic policymaker who served as United States secretary of the treasury from 2009 to 2013.

11. **Robert Gilpin (b. 1930)** is professor emeritus of politics and international affairs at Princeton University. His work focuses on the international aspects of political economy.

12. **Daniel Kahneman (b. 1934)** is professor emeritus of psychology and public affairs at Princeton University. He researched empirical data (data verifiable by

observation) to challenge the view of "rational" decision-making so popular in economic theory, making him an esteemed figure within behavioral economics.

13. **Robert Keohane (b. 1941)** is a professor of political science at Princeton University. His work built upon that of Charles P. Kindleberger, leading to new ideas about "hegemonic stability."

14. **John Maynard Keynes (1883–1946)** was an English economist whose macroeconomic theories radically changed the subject and formed the basis for today's "Keynesian school" of economics.

15. **Paul Krugman (b. 1953)** is an American Nobel Prize-winning economist whose primary subject has been international trade and the geographic distribution of economic activity.

16. **Burton G. Malkiel (b. 1932)** is an American academic, investor, and writer. He is the author of *A Random Walk Down Wall Street* (1973) and an emeritus professor at Princeton University.

17. **Alfred Marshall (1842–1924)** was a distinguished British economist and is credited as one of the founders of neoclassic economics.

18. **John Mauldin** is a financier, economist, author, and online commentator on the subject of financial markets and economic history.

19. **Lawrence G. McDonald** is the author of *A Colossal Failure of Common Sense: The Inside Story of the Collapse of Lehman Brothers* (2009), which details the collapse of the Lehman Brothers bank from an insider's perspective. McDonald had been a vice-president of the bank.

20. **John Stuart Mill (1806–73)** was an English economist and a notable philosopher. He made wide-ranging contributions to economics, political theory, and social theory.

21. **Patrick Minford (b. 1943)** is a British economist, and professor of applied economics at Cardiff University.

22. **Hyman Minsky (1919–96)** was a professor of economics at Washington University in St. Louis. His work focused on the nature of financial crises.

23. **Chuck Prince (b. 1950)** is an American businessman, and the former chairman

and chief executive of the multinational finance corporation Citigroup.

24. **Robert J. Shiller (b. 1946)** is a Nobel Prize-winning economist and author of *Irrational Exuberance* (2000). His work in financial economics and behavioral finance is skeptical of the efficient market hypothesis.

25. **Robert Skidelsky (b. 1939)** is a British economic historian and emeritus professor of political economy at the University of Warwick.

26. **Adam Smith (1723–90)** was a Scottish economist and philosopher who played a key role in the Scottish Enlightenment. His book *The Wealth of Nations* (1776) is often considered a founding work in the subject of economics.

27. **Robert M. Solow (b. 1924)** is a Nobel Prize-winning economist and emeritus Institute Professor in the economics department of Massachusetts Institute of Technology (MIT). He is best-known for his work on economic growth.

28. **George Soros (b. 1930)** is one of the world's wealthiest and most famous investors. He is chairman of Soros Fund Management and an open skeptic of the efficient market hypothesis.

29. **Lawrence Summers (b. 1954)** is an American economist who was US secretary of the treasury from 1999 to 2001. He was also chief economist at the World Bank from 1991 to 1993.

30. **Nassim Nicholas Taleb (b. 1960)** is a Lebanese American author and investor. His work on the nature of randomness and uncertainty has had an impact on the worlds of finance and philosophy, among other disciplines.

31. **Jonathan Tepper** is an American economist, author, and founder of Variant Perception, a macroeconomic research group.

32. **Amos Tversky (1937–96)** was a cognitive and mathematical psychologist. His most famous work connected the way the human mind handles risk to cognitive bias (which means interpreting information in a way that confirms preexisting prejudices).

33. **Vicky Ward (b. 1969)** is a British journalist and the author of *The Devil's Casino: Friendship, Betrayal, and the High Stakes Games Played Inside Lehman Brothers* (2010), which detailed the collapse of the investment bank.

 **WORKS CITED**

1. Allen, Katie. "Why is China's Stock Market in Crisis?" *Guardian*. July 8, 2015. Accessed March 21, 2016. http://www.theguardian.com/business/2015/jul/08/china-stock-market-crisis-explained.

2. W. Ashworth. *"Manias, Panics, and Crashes: A History of Financial Crises* by Charles P. Kindleberger." *Economic History Review* 32, no. 3 (August, 1979): 421–2.

3. Babkar, Mamta. "Soros: The Efficient Market Hypothesis Has Run Into Bankruptcy." *Business Insider*. Accessed March 21, 2016. http://www. businessinsider. com/financial-advisor-insights-june-26-2013-6?IR=T.

4. Buttonwood. "China's Stockmarket: The Great Leap Backward." *Economist*. Accessed March 21, 2016. http://www.economist.com/blogs/ buttonwood/ 2015/07/chinas-stockmarket.

5. Chevalier, Michel. *Lettres sur l'Amérique du Nord*. Brussels: Société belge du librairie, 1838.

6. Clark, Peter, Natalia Tamirisa, and Shang-Jin Wei, with Azim Sadikov, and Li Zeng. "Exchange Rate Volatility and Trade Flows — Some New Evidence." International Monetary Fund, May 2004. Accessed March 21, 2016. https://www. imf.org/ external/np/res/exrate/2004/eng/051904.pdf.

7. Cooper, Richard, Barry Eichengreen, Gerald Holtham, Robert Putnam and Randall Henning. *Can Nations Agree? Issues in International Economic Cooperation*. Washington, DC: Brookings Institution Press, 1989.

8. *Economist*. "Of Manias, Panics, and Crashes." July 17, 2003. Accessed March 21, 2016. http://www.economist.com/node/1923462.

9. Fosler, Gail. "Lessons from Kindleberger on the Financial Crisis." *The Gail Fosler Group*. April 28, 2013. Accessed March 21, 2016. http://www.gailfosler. com/ lessons-from-kindleberger-on-the-financial-crisis.

10. Geithner, Timothy F. "Change and Challenges Facing the US Financial System." New York Bankers Association's Annual Financial Services Forum, *BIS Review* 18 (March, 2004).

11. ____. *Stress Test: Reflections on Financial Crises*. New York: Crown Publishers, 2014.

12. Gekas, Sakis. "Different Because Worse." *Dublin Review of Books* 16 (Winter 2010). Accessed March 21, 2016. http://www.drb.ie/essays/different-because-worse.

13. Gilpin, Robert. *The Political Economy of International Relations*. Princeton: Princeton University Press, 1987.

14. Hakes, David R. and David C. Rose. "The 1979–1982 Monetary Policy Experiment: Monetarist, Anti-Monetarist, or Quasi-Monetarist?" *Journal of Post Keynesian Economics* 15, no. 2 (Winter 1992–3): 281–8.

15. Hutton, Will. "Why are we looking on helplessly as markets crash all over the world?" *Guardian*, January 17, 2016. Accessed March 21, 2016. http://www.theguardian.com/commentisfree/2016/jan/17/china-economic-crisis-world-economy-global-capitalism.

16. Ishikawa, Tetsuya. *How I Caused the Credit Crunch: An Insider's Story of the Financial Meltdown*. London: Icon Books, 2009.

17. Joyce, Joseph P. "The Enduring Relevance of 'Manias, Panics, and Crashes.'" *Capital Ebbs and Flows*. Accessed March 21, 2016. https://blogs.wellesley.edu/jjoyce/2015/12/14/the-enduring-relevance-of-manias-panics-and-crashes-2/.

18. Keohane, Robert. *After Hegemony: Cooperation and Discord in the World of Political Economy*. Princeton: Princeton University Press, 1984.

19. Kindleberger, Charles P. *The Dollar Shortage*. New York: John Wiley & Sons, 1950.

20. ____. *International Short-term Capital Movements*. New York: Columbia University Press, 1937.

21. ____. *The World in Depression, 1929–1939*. Berkeley; Los Angeles: University of California Press, 1973.

22. ____. *The World in Depression, 1929–1939*. Edited by J. Bradford DeLong and Barry Eichengreen. Berkeley: University of California Press, 2013.

23. Kindleberger. Charles P. and Robert Z. Aliber. *Manias, Panics, and Crashes: A History of Financial Crises*. London: Palgrave MacMillan, 2015.

24. Kirkup, James. "Gordon Brown admits he was wrong to claim he had ended 'boom and bust.'" *Telegraph*, November 21, 2008. Accessed March 21, 2016. http://www.telegraph.co.uk/finance/recession/3497533/Gordon-Brown-admits-he-was-wrong-to-claim-he-had-ended-boom-and-bust.html

25. Knoop, Todd A. *Business Cycle Economics: Understanding Recessions and Depressions from Boom to Bust*. Santa Barbara, CA: Praeger, 2015.

26. Kobrak, Christopher and Mira Wilkins, ed. *History and Financial Crisis: Lessons from the 20th Century*. New York: Routledge, 2013.

27. Krugman, Paul and Robin Wells. "The Busts Keep Getting Bigger: Why?" *New York Review of Books*, July 14, 2011. Accessed March 21, 2016. http://www.nybooks.com/articles/2011/07/14/busts-keep-getting-bigger-why/

28. Krugman, Paul. "China Bites the Cherry." *New York Times*, August 12, 2015. Accessed March 21, 2016. http://krugman.blogs.nytimes.com/2015/08/12/ china-bites-the-cherry/?_r=0.

29. ____. "Why We Regulate." *New York Times*, May 13, 2012. Accessed March 21, 2016. http://www.nytimes.com/2012/05/14/opinion/krugman-why-we-regulate.html.

30. Lewitt, Michael. "Oil is Going to Fall by 50%... Again." Michael Lewitt's Sure Money, September 28, 2015. Accessed on January 17, 2016. http://suremoneyinvestor.com/2015/09/oil-is-going-to-fall-by-50-again/.

31. McDonald, Lawrence G. and Patrick Robinson. *A Colossal Failure of Common Sense: The Inside Story of the Collapse of Lehman Brothers*. New York: Three Rivers Press, 2009.

32. Malkiel, Burton G. "The Efficient Market Hypothesis and Its Critics." *Journal of Economic Perspectives*, 17, no. 1 (Winter, 2003): 59–82.

33. ____. *A Random Walk Down Wall Street: The Time-Tested Strategy for Successful Investing*. New York: W.W. Norton & Company, 2015.

34. Maudlin, John and Jonathan Tepper. *Code Red: How to Protect Your Savings From the Coming Crisis*. Hoboken: John Wiley & Sons, 2013.

35. Meardon, Stephen. "On Kindleberger and Hegemony: From Berlin to M.I.T. and Back." Bowdoin Digital Commons, September 29, 2013. Accessed March 21, 2016. http://digitalcommons.bowdoin.edu/cgi/viewcontent.cgi?article=1003&con text=econpapers.

36. Minford, Patrick. *"Manias, Panics, and Crashes. A History of Financial Crises. By Charles P. Kindleberger." Economic Journal* 89 (December, 1979).

37. Mody, Ashoka. "Germany must lead by example on fixing its banks." *Financial Times*, May 27, 2013. Accessed March 21, 2016. http://www.ft.com/intl/cms/s/0/10e7ccbe-c46f-11e2-9ac0-00144feab7de.html#axzz43Y4Huy4b.

38. Murray, Nick. "A Treasure Trove of Financial Folly." *Financial Advisor*, January 1, 2016. Accessed March 24, 2016. http://www.fa-mag.com/news/a-treasure-trove- of-financial-folly-24440.html.

39. Pasotti, Piero and Alessandro Vercelli. "Kindleberger and Financial Crises." *Financialisation, Economy, Society, and Sustainable Development Working Paper Series* 104, February 2015. Accessed March 21, 2016. http://fessud.eu/wp-content/uploads/2015/01/Kindleberger-and-Financial-Crises-Fessud-final_Working-Paper-104.pdf.

40. Patterson, Scott. *The Quants: How a New Breed of Math Whizzes Conquered Wall Street and Nearly Destroyed It*. New York: Crown Business, 2010.

41. Sheng, Andres and Xiao Geng. "China's Live Stress Test." *Project Syndicate: The World's Opinion Page*. July 21, 2015. Accessed March 21, 2016. http://www.project-syndicate.org/commentary/china-stock-market-government-intervention-by-andrew-sheng-and-xiao-geng-2015-07?barrier=true.

42. Shiller, Robert J. *Irrational Exuberance*. Princeton: Princeton University Press, 2015.

43. Sylla, Richard. "Financial Disturbances and Depressions: The View from Economic History." Social Science Research Network: Levy Economics Institute Working Paper 47 (April, 1991).

44. Taleb, Nassim Nicholas. *The Black Swan: The Impact of the Highly Improbable*. London: Penguin, 2007.

45. Turk, Michael H. *The Idea of History in Constructing Economics*. Abingdon: Routledge, 2016.

46. Ward, Vicky. *The Devil's Casino: Friendship, Betrayal, and the High-Stakes Games Played Inside Lehman Brothers*. Hoboken: John Wiley & Sons, 2010.

47. Westbrook, David. *City of Gold: An Apology for Global Capitalism in a Time of Discontent*. New York: Routledge, 2004.

48. Zweig, Jason. "Read It and Reap: The Best Books for Investors." *Wall Street Journal.* November 28, 2015. Accessed March 21, 2016. http://www.wsj.com/articles/read-it-and-reap-the-best-books-for-investors-1417213387.

原书作者简介

查尔斯·P.金德尔伯格于1910年出生于纽约市。他学习经济学时正值20世纪30年代的大萧条期间，在这一场剧烈的金融危机之后，是一个前所未有的艰难时期——尤其对美国来说。金德尔伯格参加了第二次世界大战，战后帮助起草了马歇尔计划，这是一项美国的经济战略，在财政上支持战后重建欧洲。这些经历塑造了他的职业生涯和思想，让他试图去探究金融危机的真正原因；这些金融危机还暴露了全球化世界中各个国家经济之间的重要联系。他于2003年去世，享年92岁。金德尔伯格被誉为世界经济学界的重要人物。

本书作者简介

尼克·伯顿博士拥有经济学和文学双重学位。他目前在牛津和伦敦任教。

世界名著中的批判性思维

《世界思想宝库钥匙丛书》致力于深入浅出地阐释全世界著名思想家的观点，不论是谁、在何处都能了解到，从而推进批判性思维发展。

《世界思想宝库钥匙丛书》与世界顶尖大学的一流学者合作，为一系列学科中最有影响的著作推出新的分析文本，介绍其观点和影响。在这一不断扩展的系列中，每种选入的著作都代表了历经时间考验的思想典范。通过为这些著作提供必要背景、揭示原作者的学术渊源以及说明这些著作所产生的影响，本系列图书希望让读者以新视角看待这些划时代的经典之作。读者应学会思考、运用并挑战这些著作中的观点，而不是简单接受它们。

ABOUT THE AUTHOR OF THE ORIGINAL WORK

Charles P. Kindleberger was born in New York City in 1910. He studied economics during the Great Depression of the 1930s, which followed a dramatic financial crash and was a time of unprecedented hardship — particularly in America. Kindleberger fought in World War II, and helped draft the Marshall Plan, an economic strategy that saw the US financially support the postwar rebuilding of Europe. These experiences shaped his career and thinking, as he tried to understand the real reasons for financial crises; they also exposed the crucial connections between national economies in a globalized world. When he died in 2003 at the age of 92, Kindleberger was hailed as a major figure in the world of economics.

ABOUT THE AUTHOR OF THE ANALYSIS

Dr Nick Burton holds degrees in both economics and literature. He currently lectures in Oxford and London.

ABOUT MACAT
GREAT WORKS FOR CRITICAL THINKING

Macat is focused on making the ideas of the world's great thinkers accessible and comprehensible to everybody, everywhere, in ways that promote the development of enhanced critical thinking skills.

It works with leading academics from the world's top universities to produce new analyses that focus on the ideas and the impact of the most influential works ever written across a wide variety of academic disciplines. Each of the works that sit at the heart of its growing library is an enduring example of great thinking. But by setting them in context — and looking at the influences that shaped their authors, as well as the responses they provoked — Macat encourages readers to look at these classics and game-changers with fresh eyes. Readers learn to think, engage and challenge their ideas, rather than simply accepting them.

批判性思维与《疯狂、惊恐和崩溃》

首要批判性思维技巧：评估

次要批判性思维技巧：理性化思维

　　查尔斯·金德尔伯格的经典著作《疯狂、惊恐和崩溃》特别关注金融泡沫，而金融泡沫最奇怪的特征可能就是那些被困在其中的人从来没有能力理解他们困境的严重性。他们原则上知道泡沫的存在，知道泡沫造成的金融危机能够摧毁个人财富和整个经济。然而，无论何时何地泡沫开始形成，人们都被告知，这一次情况有所不同，还是有充分的理由继续投资，并假定价格会永远、稳定、持续地上涨。

　　金德尔伯格的成就就是运用批判性思维中的评估来检验这种奇怪的心态，以及支持这种心态而提出的论点。他严厉地评判了产生这种论点的理由的可接受度，强调其推理的相关性和充分性问题，让我们有充分的理由怀疑这些论点。金德尔伯格还运用他的理性化思维达成了一个不寻常的成就，那就是虽然他写的是专业的经济学著作，却可以让非专家读者理解和相信其论点的正确性。

CRITICAL THINKING AND *MANIAS, PANICS, AND CRASHES*

- Primary critical thinking skill: EVALUATION
- Secondary critical thinking skill: REASONING

Perhaps the most peculiar feature of a financial bubble—one that Charles Kindleberger's classic work *Manias, Panics, and Crashes* draws particular attention to—is the inability of those trapped inside it to grasp the seriousness of their predicament. They know in principle that bubbles exist, and they know that the financial crashes that result from them are capable of destroying individuals' wealth and entire economies. Yet whenever and wherever a bubble begins to form, we're told that this time things are different, that there are sound reasons to continue to invest and to presume that prices will continue to rise steadily forever.

Kindleberger's achievement is to use the critical thinking skill of evaluation to examine this strange mindset and the arguments advanced in support of it. He harshly judges the acceptability of the reasons used to create such arguments, and highlights the issues of relevance and adequacy that give us every reason to doubt them. Kindleberger also uses his powers of reasoning to effect an unusual achievement—writing a work soundly rooted in economics that nonetheless engages and convinces a non-specialist audience of the correctness of his arguments.

《世界思想宝库钥匙丛书》简介

《世界思想宝库钥匙丛书》致力于为一系列在各领域产生重大影响的人文社科类经典著作提供独特的学术探讨。每一本读物都不仅仅是原经典著作的内容摘要，而是介绍并深入研究原经典著作的学术渊源、主要观点和历史影响。这一丛书的目的是提供一套学习资料，以促进读者掌握批判性思维，从而更全面、深刻地去理解重要思想。

每一本读物分为3个部分：学术渊源、学术思想和学术影响，每个部分下有4个小节。这些章节旨在从各个方面研究原经典著作及其反响。

由于独特的体例，每一本读物不但易于阅读，而且另有一项优点：所有读物的编排体例相同，读者在进行某个知识层面的调查或研究时可交叉参阅多本该丛书中的相关读物，从而开启跨领域研究的路径。

为了方便阅读，每本读物最后还列出了术语表和人名表（在书中则以星号 * 标记），此外还有参考文献。

《世界思想宝库钥匙丛书》与剑桥大学合作，理清了批判性思维的要点，即如何通过6种技能来进行有效思考。其中3种技能让我们能够理解问题，另3种技能让我们有能力解决问题。这6种技能合称为"批判性思维PACIER模式"，它们是：

分析：了解如何建立一个观点；

评估：研究一个观点的优点和缺点；

阐释：对意义所产生的问题加以理解；

创造性思维：提出新的见解，发现新的联系；

解决问题：提出切实有效的解决办法；

理性化思维：创建有说服力的观点。

THE MACAT LIBRARY

The Macat Library is a series of unique academic explorations of seminal works in the humanities and social sciences — books and papers that have had a significant and widely recognised impact on their disciplines. It has been created to serve as much more than just a summary of what lies between the covers of a great book. It illuminates and explores the influences on, ideas of, and impact of that book. Our goal is to offer a learning resource that encourages critical thinking and fosters a better, deeper understanding of important ideas.

Each publication is divided into three Sections: Influences, Ideas, and Impact. Each Section has four Modules. These explore every important facet of the work, and the responses to it.

This Section-Module structure makes a Macat Library book easy to use, but it has another important feature. Because each Macat book is written to the same format, it is possible (and encouraged!) to cross-reference multiple Macat books along the same lines of inquiry or research. This allows the reader to open up interesting interdisciplinary pathways.

To further aid your reading, lists of glossary terms and people mentioned are included at the end of this book (these are indicated by an asterisk [*] throughout) — as well as a list of works cited.

Macat has worked with the University of Cambridge to identify the elements of critical thinking and understand the ways in which six different skills combine to enable effective thinking.

Three allow us to fully understand a problem; three more give us the tools to solve it. Together, these six skills make up the PACIER model of critical thinking. They are:

ANALYSIS — understanding how an argument is built
EVALUATION — exploring the strengths and weaknesses of an argument
INTERPRETATION — understanding issues of meaning
CREATIVE THINKING — coming up with new ideas and fresh connections
PROBLEM-SOLVING — producing strong solutions
REASONING — creating strong arguments

"《世界思想宝库钥匙丛书》提供了独一无二的跨学科学习和研究工具。它介绍那些革新了各自学科研究的经典著作，还邀请全世界一流专家和教育机构进行严谨的分析，为每位读者打开世界顶级教育的大门。"

—— 安德烈亚斯·施莱歇尔，
经济合作与发展组织教育与技能司司长

"《世界思想宝库钥匙丛书》直面大学教育的巨大挑战……他们组建了一支精干而活跃的学者队伍，来推出在研究广度上颇具新意的教学材料。"

—— 布罗尔斯教授、勋爵，剑桥大学前校长

"《世界思想宝库钥匙丛书》的愿景令人赞叹。它通过分析和阐释那些曾深刻影响人类思想以及社会、经济发展的经典文本，提供了新的学习方法。它推动批判性思维，这对于任何社会和经济体来说都是至关重要的。这就是未来的学习方法。"

—— 查尔斯·克拉克阁下，英国前教育大臣

"对于那些影响了各自领域的著作，《世界思想宝库钥匙丛书》能让人们立即了解到围绕那些著作展开的评论性言论，这让该系列图书成为在这些领域从事研究的师生们不可或缺的资源。"

—— 威廉·特朗佐教授，加利福尼亚大学圣地亚哥分校

"Macat offers an amazing first-of-its-kind tool for interdisciplinary learning and research. Its focus on works that transformed their disciplines and its rigorous approach, drawing on the world's leading experts and educational institutions, opens up a world-class education to anyone."

—— Andreas Schleicher, Director for Education and Skills, Organisation for Economic Co-operation and Development

"Macat is taking on some of the major challenges in university education... They have drawn together a strong team of active academics who are producing teaching materials that are novel in the breadth of their approach."

—— Prof Lord Broers, former Vice-Chancellor of the University of Cambridge

"The Macat vision is exceptionally exciting. It focuses upon new modes of learning which analyse and explain seminal texts which have profoundly influenced world thinking and so social and economic development. It promotes the kind of critical thinking which is essential for any society and economy. This is the learning of the future."

—— Rt Hon Charles Clarke, former UK Secretary of State for Education

"The Macat analyses provide immediate access to the critical conversation surrounding the books that have shaped their respective discipline, which will make them an invaluable resource to all of those, students and teachers, working in the field."

—— Prof William Tronzo, University of California at San Diego

The Macat Library
世界思想宝库钥匙丛书

TITLE	中文书名	类别
An Analysis of Arjun Appadurai's *Modernity at Large: Cultural Dimensions of Globalization*	解析阿尔君·阿帕杜莱《消失的现代性：全球化的文化维度》	人类学
An Analysis of Claude Lévi-Strauss's *Structural Anthropology*	解析克劳德·列维–斯特劳斯《结构人类学》	人类学
An Analysis of Marcel Mauss's *The Gift*	解析马塞尔·莫斯《礼物》	人类学
An Analysis of Jared M. Diamond's *Guns, Germs, and Steel: The Fate of Human Societies*	解析贾雷德·M.戴蒙德《枪炮、病菌与钢铁：人类社会的命运》	人类学
An Analysis of Clifford Geertz's *The Interpretation of Cultures*	解析克利福德·格尔茨《文化的解释》	人类学
An Analysis of Philippe Ariès's *Centuries of Childhood: A Social History of Family Life*	解析菲力浦·阿利埃斯《儿童的世纪：旧制度下的儿童和家庭生活》	人类学
An Analysis of W. Chan Kim & Renée Mauborgne's *Blue Ocean Strategy*	解析金伟灿/勒妮·莫博涅《蓝海战略》	商业
An Analysis of John P. Kotter's *Leading Change*	解析约翰·P.科特《领导变革》	商业
An Analysis of Michael E. Porter's *Competitive Strategy: Techniques for Analyzing Industries and Competitors*	解析迈克尔·E.波特《竞争战略：分析产业和竞争对手的技术》	商业
An Analysis of Jean Lave & Etienne Wenger's *Situated Learning: Legitimate Peripheral Participation*	解析琼·莱夫/艾蒂纳·温格《情境学习：合法的边缘性参与》	商业
An Analysis of Douglas McGregor's *The Human Side of Enterprise*	解析道格拉斯·麦格雷戈《企业的人性面》	商业
An Analysis of Milton Friedman's *Capitalism and Freedom*	解析米尔顿·弗里德曼《资本主义与自由》	商业
An Analysis of Ludwig von Mises's *The Theory of Money and Credit*	解析路德维希·冯·米塞斯《货币和信用理论》	经济学
An Analysis of Adam Smith's *The Wealth of Nations*	解析亚当·斯密《国富论》	经济学
An Analysis of Thomas Piketty's *Capital in the Twenty-First Century*	解析托马斯·皮凯蒂《21世纪资本论》	经济学
An Analysis of Nassim Nicholas Taleb's *The Black Swan: The Impact of the Highly Improbable*	解析纳西姆·尼古拉斯·塔勒布《黑天鹅：如何应对不可预知的未来》	经济学
An Analysis of Ha-Joon Chang's *Kicking Away the Ladder*	解析张夏准《富国陷阱：发达国家为何踢开梯子》	经济学
An Analysis of Thomas Robert Malthus's *An Essay on the Principle of Population*	解析托马斯·罗伯特·马尔萨斯《人口论》	经济学

An Analysis of John Maynard Keynes's *The General Theory of Employment, Interest and Money*	解析约翰·梅纳德·凯恩斯《就业、利息和货币通论》	经济学
An Analysis of Milton Friedman's *The Role of Monetary Policy*	解析米尔顿·弗里德曼《货币政策的作用》	经济学
An Analysis of Burton G. Malkiel's *A Random Walk Down Wall Street*	解析伯顿·G.马尔基尔《漫步华尔街》	经济学
An Analysis of Friedrich A. Hayek's *The Road to Serfdom*	解析弗里德里希·A.哈耶克《通往奴役之路》	经济学
An Analysis of Charles P. Kindleberger's *Manias, Panics, and Crashes: A History of Financial Crises*	解析查尔斯·P.金德尔伯格《疯狂、惊恐和崩溃：金融危机史》	经济学
An Analysis of Amartya Sen's *Development as Freedom*	解析阿马蒂亚·森《以自由看待发展》	经济学
An Analysis of Rachel Carson's *Silent Spring*	解析蕾切尔·卡森《寂静的春天》	地理学
An Analysis of Charles Darwin's *On the Origin of Species: by Means of Natural Selection, or The Preservation of Favoured Races in the Struggle for Life*	解析查尔斯·达尔文《物种起源》	地理学
An Analysis of World Commission on Environment and Development's *The Brundtland Report, Our Common Future*	解析世界环境与发展委员会《布伦特兰报告：我们共同的未来》	地理学
An Analysis of James E. Lovelock's *Gaia: A New Look at Life on Earth*	解析詹姆斯·E.拉伍洛克《盖娅：地球生命的新视野》	地理学
An Analysis of Paul Kennedy's *The Rise and Fall of the Great Powers: Economic Change and Military Conflict from 1500–2000*	解析保罗·肯尼迪《大国的兴衰：1500—2000年的经济变革与军事冲突》	历史
An Analysis of Janet L. Abu-Lughod's *Before European Hegemony: The World System A. D. 1250–1350*	解析珍妮特·L.阿布-卢格霍德《欧洲霸权之前：1250—1350年的世界体系》	历史
An Analysis of Alfred W. Crosby's *The Columbian Exchange: Biological and Cultural Consequences of 1492*	解析艾尔弗雷德·W.克罗斯比《哥伦布大交换：1492年以后的生物影响和文化冲击》	历史
An Analysis of Tony Judt's *Postwar: A History of Europe since 1945*	解析托尼·朱特《战后欧洲史》	历史
An Analysis of Richard J. Evans's *In Defence of History*	解析理查德·J.艾文斯《捍卫历史》	历史
An Analysis of Eric Hobsbawm's *The Age of Revolution: Europe 1789–1848*	解析艾瑞克·霍布斯鲍姆《革命的年代：欧洲1789—1848年》	历史

An Analysis of Roland Barthes's *Mythologies*	解析罗兰·巴特《神话学》	文学与批判理论
An Analysis of Simone de Beauvoir's *The Second Sex*	解析西蒙娜·德·波伏娃《第二性》	文学与批判理论
An Analysis of Edward W. Said's *Orientalism*	解析爱德华·W.萨义德《东方主义》	文学与批判理论
An Analysis of Virginia Woolf's *A Room of One's Own*	解析弗吉尼亚·伍尔芙《一间自己的房间》	文学与批判理论
An Analysis of Judith Butler's *Gender Trouble*	解析朱迪斯·巴特勒《性别麻烦》	文学与批判理论
An Analysis of Ferdinand de Saussure's *Course in General Linguistics*	解析费尔迪南·德·索绪尔《普通语言学教程》	文学与批判理论
An Analysis of Susan Sontag's *On Photography*	解析苏珊·桑塔格《论摄影》	文学与批判理论
An Analysis of Walter Benjamin's *The Work of Art in the Age of Mechanical Reproduction*	解析瓦尔特·本雅明《机械复制时代的艺术作品》	文学与批判理论
An Analysis of W. E. B. Du Bois's *The Souls of Black Folk*	解析W.E.B.杜波依斯《黑人的灵魂》	文学与批判理论
An Analysis of Plato's *The Republic*	解析柏拉图《理想国》	哲学
An Analysis of Plato's *Symposium*	解析柏拉图《会饮篇》	哲学
An Analysis of Aristotle's *Metaphysics*	解析亚里士多德《形而上学》	哲学
An Analysis of Aristotle's *Nicomachean Ethics*	解析亚里士多德《尼各马可伦理学》	哲学
An Analysis of Immanuel Kant's *Critique of Pure Reason*	解析伊曼努尔·康德《纯粹理性批判》	哲学
An Analysis of Ludwig Wittgenstein's *Philosophical Investigations*	解析路德维希·维特根斯坦《哲学研究》	哲学
An Analysis of G. W. F. Hegel's *Phenomenology of Spirit*	解析G.W.F.黑格尔《精神现象学》	哲学
An Analysis of Baruch Spinoza's *Ethics*	解析巴鲁赫·斯宾诺莎《伦理学》	哲学
An Analysis of Hannah Arendt's *The Human Condition*	解析汉娜·阿伦特《人的境况》	哲学
An Analysis of G. E. M. Anscombe's *Modern Moral Philosophy*	解析G.E.M.安斯康姆《现代道德哲学》	哲学
An Analysis of David Hume's *An Enquiry Concerning Human Understanding*	解析大卫·休谟《人类理解研究》	哲学

An Analysis of Søren Kierkegaard's *Fear and Trembling*	解析索伦·克尔凯郭尔《恐惧与战栗》	哲学
An Analysis of René Descartes's *Meditations on First Philosophy*	解析勒内·笛卡尔《第一哲学沉思录》	哲学
An Analysis of Friedrich Nietzsche's *On the Genealogy of Morality*	解析弗里德里希·尼采《论道德的谱系》	哲学
An Analysis of Gilbert Ryle's *The Concept of Mind*	解析吉尔伯特·赖尔《心的概念》	哲学
An Analysis of Thomas Kuhn's *The Structure of Scientific Revolutions*	解析托马斯·库恩《科学革命的结构》	哲学
An Analysis of John Stuart Mill's *Utilitarianism*	解析约翰·斯图亚特·穆勒《功利主义》	哲学
An Analysis of Aristotle's *Politics*	解析亚里士多德《政治学》	政治学
An Analysis of Niccolò Machiavelli's *The Prince*	解析尼科洛·马克雅维利《君主论》	政治学
An Analysis of Karl Marx's *Capital*	解析卡尔·马克思《资本论》	政治学
An Analysis of Benedict Anderson's *Imagined Communities*	解析本尼迪克特·安德森《想象的共同体》	政治学
An Analysis of Samuel P. Huntington's *The Clash of Civilizations and the Remaking of World Order*	解析塞缪尔·P.亨廷顿《文明的冲突与世界秩序的重建》	政治学
An Analysis of Alexis de Tocqueville's *Democracy in America*	解析阿列克西·德·托克维尔《论美国的民主》	政治学
An Analysis of John A. Hobson's *Imperialism: A Study*	解析约翰·A.霍布森《帝国主义》	政治学
An Analysis of Thomas Paine's *Common Sense*	解析托马斯·潘恩《常识》	政治学
An Analysis of John Rawls's *A Theory of Justice*	解析约翰·罗尔斯《正义论》	政治学
An Analysis of Francis Fukuyama's *The End of History and the Last Man*	解析弗朗西斯·福山《历史的终结与最后的人》	政治学
An Analysis of John Locke's *Two Treatises of Government*	解析约翰·洛克《政府论》	政治学
An Analysis of Sun Tzu's *The Art of War*	解析孙武《孙子兵法》	政治学
An Analysis of Henry Kissinger's *World Order: Reflections on the Character of Nations and the Course of History*	解析亨利·基辛格《世界秩序》	政治学
An Analysis of Jean-Jacques Rousseau's *The Social Contract*	解析让-雅克·卢梭《社会契约论》	政治学

An Analysis of Odd Arne Westad's *The Global Cold War: Third World Interventions and the Making of Our Times*	解析文安立《全球冷战：美苏对第三世界的干涉与当代世界的形成》	政治学
An Analysis of Sigmund Freud's *The Interpretation of Dreams*	解析西格蒙德·弗洛伊德《梦的解析》	心理学
An Analysis of William James' *The Principles of Psychology*	解析威廉·詹姆斯《心理学原理》	心理学
An Analysis of Philip Zimbardo's *The Lucifer Effect*	解析菲利普·津巴多《路西法效应》	心理学
An Analysis of Leon Festinger's *A Theory of Cognitive Dissonance*	解析利昂·费斯汀格《认知失调论》	心理学
An Analysis of Richard H. Thaler & Cass R. Sunstein's *Nudge: Improving Decisions about Health, Wealth, and Happiness*	解析理查德·H. 泰勒 / 卡斯·R. 桑斯坦《助推：如何做出有关健康、财富和幸福的更优决策》	心理学
An Analysis of Gordon Allport's *The Nature of Prejudice*	解析高尔登·奥尔波特《偏见的本质》	心理学
An Analysis of Steven Pinker's *The Better Angels of Our Nature: Why Violence Has Declined*	解析斯蒂芬·平克《人性中的善良天使：暴力为什么会减少》	心理学
An Analysis of Stanley Milgram's *Obedience to Authority*	解析斯坦利·米尔格拉姆《对权威的服从》	心理学
An Analysis of Betty Friedan's *The Feminine Mystique*	解析贝蒂·弗里丹《女性的奥秘》	心理学
An Analysis of David Riesman's *The Lonely Crowd: A Study of the Changing American Character*	解析大卫·理斯曼《孤独的人群：美国人社会性格演变之研究》	社会学
An Analysis of Franz Boas's *Race, Language and Culture*	解析弗朗兹·博厄斯《种族、语言与文化》	社会学
An Analysis of Pierre Bourdieu's *Outline of a Theory of Practice*	解析皮埃尔·布尔迪厄《实践理论大纲》	社会学
An Analysis of Max Weber's *The Protestant Ethic and the Spirit of Capitalism*	解析马克斯·韦伯《新教伦理与资本主义精神》	社会学
An Analysis of Jane Jacobs's *The Death and Life of Great American Cities*	解析简·雅各布斯《美国大城市的死与生》	社会学
An Analysis of C. Wright Mills's *The Sociological Imagination*	解析 C. 赖特·米尔斯《社会学的想象力》	社会学
An Analysis of Robert E. Lucas Jr.'s *Why Doesn't Capital Flow from Rich to Poor Countries?*	解析小罗伯特·E. 卢卡斯《为何资本不从富国流向穷国？》	社会学

An Analysis of Émile Durkheim's *On Suicide*	解析埃米尔·迪尔凯姆《自杀论》	社会学
An Analysis of Eric Hoffer's *The True Believer: Thoughts on the Nature of Mass Movements*	解析埃里克·霍弗《狂热分子：群众运动圣经》	社会学
An Analysis of Jared M. Diamond's *Collapse: How Societies Choose to Fail or Survive*	解析贾雷德·M.戴蒙德《大崩溃：社会如何选择兴亡》	社会学
An Analysis of Michel Foucault's *The History of Sexuality Vol. 1: The Will to Knowledge*	解析米歇尔·福柯《性史（第一卷）：求知意志》	社会学
An Analysis of Michel Foucault's *Discipline and Punish*	解析米歇尔·福柯《规训与惩罚》	社会学
An Analysis of Richard Dawkins's *The Selfish Gene*	解析理查德·道金斯《自私的基因》	社会学
An Analysis of Antonio Gramsci's *Prison Notebooks*	解析安东尼奥·葛兰西《狱中札记》	社会学
An Analysis of Augustine's *Confessions*	解析奥古斯丁《忏悔录》	神学
An Analysis of C. S. Lewis's *The Abolition of Man*	解析 C. S. 路易斯《人之废》	神学

图书在版编目（CIP）数据

解析查尔斯·P.金德尔伯格《疯狂、惊恐和崩溃：金融危机史》：汉、英／尼克·伯顿（Nick Burton）著；陈汉敏译.—上海：上海外语教育出版社，2020
（世界思想宝库钥匙丛书）
ISBN 978-7-5446-6393-9

Ⅰ.①解… Ⅱ.①尼… ②陈… Ⅲ.①金融危机－经济史－研究－世界－汉、英 Ⅳ.①F831.9 ②F831.59

中国版本图书馆CIP数据核字（2020）第056434号

图字：09 – 2018 – 549

出版发行：**上海外语教育出版社**
　　　　　（上海外国语大学内）　邮编：200083
电　　话：021-65425300（总机）
电子邮箱：bookinfo@sflep.com.cn
网　　址：http://www.sflep.com
责任编辑：杨莹雪

印　　刷：上海叶大印务发展有限公司
开　　本：890×1240　1/32　印张 6　字数 123千字
版　　次：2020 年 6 月第 1 版　　2020 年 6 月第 1 次印刷
印　　数：2 100 册

书　　号：ISBN 978-7-5446-6393-9
定　　价：30.00 元
　　　　本版图书如有印装质量问题，可向本社调换
　　　　质量服务热线：4008-213-263　电子邮箱：editorial@sflep.com